I0837246

Calvin Coleman is a very talented creative artist whose work is very multilayered and multi -textured. The messages reflected in his paintings go beyond the visual and straight to the heart of the viewer. His incredible use of 'thick frothy texture' gives his paintings an even greater visual appeal. For collectors who missed the opportunity to acquire work by some of the most sought after artists of the 1990s, Calvin's work gives you a second chance.

It is phenomenal!

— *Thelma Harris, Director*
Thelma Harris Art Gallery
Oakland, California

COLEMAN
His Art Story

CALVIN COLEMAN
WITH KARSONYA WISE WHITEHEAD

COLEMAN

His Art Story

CALVIN COLEMAN

WITH KARSONYA WISE WHITEHEAD

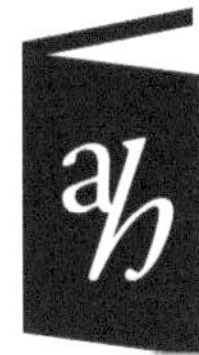

Apprentice House Press
Loyola University Maryland
Baltimore, Maryland
www.ApprenticeHouse.com

First Edition

Printed in the United States of America

ISBN: 978-1-62720-109-4

Design by Apprentice House

Cover painting:
Encore - 48 x 24in, Acrylic Mixed Media on Canvas

Published by Apprentice House

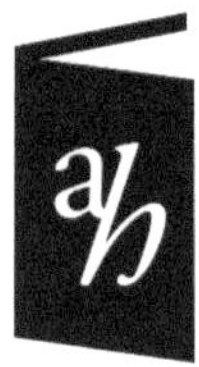

Apprentice House Press
Loyola University Maryland
4501 N. Charles Street
Baltimore, MD 21210
410.617.5265 • 410.617.2198 (fax)
www.ApprenticeHouse.com
info@ApprenticeHouse.com

DEDICATION

In memory of my oldest son, Christopher Smith Coleman (1993-2013)

&

To the future of my youngest son, Noah Coleman

CONTENTS

INTRODUCTION

The work of Calvin Coleman II is both inspiring and spiritually uplifting. Through his powerful imagery he reminds us that peace and comfort can be found in the Word of God. Coleman is a self-taught painter who builds upon his canvas with an assemblage of heavy body acrylic paint, a variety of textiles and other media to embellish his uninhibited and grandly expressive compositions. In *Art Matters*, January 2007, art critic Wuanda Walls stated that Calvin's work is "endowed with an aura of originality and poetic whimsy."

Calvin was born in Hampton, Virginia in 1966. He spent his adolescent years in Swarthmore, Pennsylvania, a Philadelphia suburb. After graduating from Lincoln University, where he earned his B.S. degree in Early Childhood Education, he began teaching at the elementary school level. During this period, Calvin began creating art as a hobby. It was upon selling his first painting, a portrait of Harriett Tubman, that he discovered his gift as an artist. In 2004, he began his professional art career creating art career. He used it to teach others about the love and power of God.

Many of Coleman's works are inspired by his personal journey and spiritual beliefs which transcend culture and creed. His mission is to impact the world with his creative vision and to touch the soul of the observer. His signature piece, "He'll Bring Me Through the Storm," was birthed out of a painful experience. In it, the Holy Spirit, symbolized by a dove, serves as a reminder that God is always there, gently guiding our path. For Calvin, the painting is a testament to his belief that with God's love, we are able to weather stormy periods victoriously.

His textured canvases embedded with bible scriptures, entice the viewer to take a close look, thus revealing subtle spiritual messages, allowing for purposeful reflection. Coleman executed this technique with great effectiveness in his 2007 Wisdom and Virtuous Woman series, bodies of work which explored a man and woman's relationship with God.

His oeuvre expands beyond the spiritual, as Calvin also draws inspiration from his love of family, music and nature's beauty. Infusing movement and color into his paintings, he captures beauty and passion. Among other themes, the artist creates abstract florals, landscapes, cityscapes, and portraits. Artists who influence his artistic style include colorist and abstract painter, Richard Mayhew for his free-form technique; and French expressionist, Chaim Soutine's dense textural characteristics.

In 2013, Coleman challenged himself to create a body of work for the blind and visually impaired. This would test his ability as an artist in ways it had never been tested before. His concern with shape, color and form produced richly textured canvases, and resulted in the series, "Do You Feel What I See?"

Rising out of his semi-abstract style, is a tension between the rough and smooth surfaces of the paintings. Mothers, fathers, sons, and daughters appear as contoured bodies, posed in dialogue, telling life's stories through undulating movements and grace.

Coleman's technique conveys a deep sensitivity toward the blind and visually impaired as he sought to enhance their experience, while providing visual interest for the seeing audience. For all, this complex body of work beckons to be touched. One's connectivity with the materials offers a meaningful encounter which enriches the soul.

Works by Calvin have been exhibited in cities and museums across the United States and abroad in Rome, Italy and Toulouse, France. His paintings are included in numerous public and private collections. Among these are the permanent collections of the City of Atlanta Housing and Urban Development; Lincoln University (PA); Drexel University; The GE Healthcare Corporate Office; the Jericho City of Praise; the Jericho Christian Academy; the Rock View Elementary School; the Patuxent Elementary School; the RIMS Center for Enrichment and Development; Tri Tech Enterprises Systems Inc.; the Global Design; the Arel Architects Inc.; the M.H. West and Co., Inc.; the Daniel Texidor Parker Collection, the Patric McCoy Collection, the Arthur Jones Collection, the Curtis Jones Collection, the Pamela Blackman Collection and the James Oliver M.D. Collection.

Commissions include: Lincoln University (mural) 2012; Verizon Wireless and Global Hue, "One Accord" 2008; Mr. Chenoa Osayande, "Muhammad Ali, Bob Marley and Malcolm X", 2005; Mr. and Mrs. Blake, "Ken and Melissa" and "Melissa and Children", 2005; and Ms. Alvah Beander, "Marvin and Blair." 2006.

—Myrtis Bedolla, Founding Director and Independent Curator
Galerie Myrtis

A MAN THINKETH

A Man Thinketh explores my process as an artist and how I work to remove myself from the world around me so that I can create a world for others to "see." I am an introvert and through my paintings I am able to speak to others.

42in x 36in
Acrylic Mixed Media on Canvas

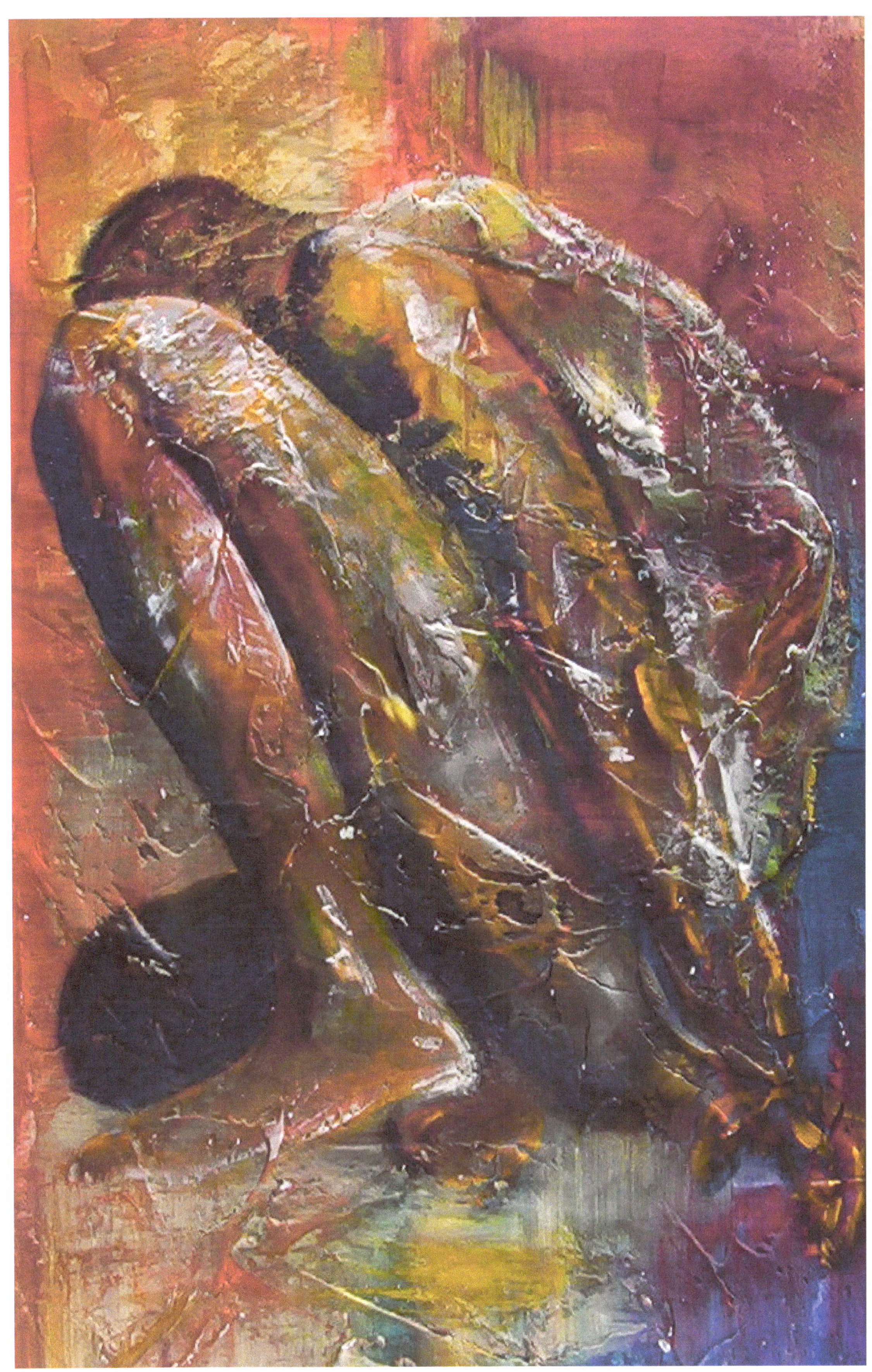

THE BOY WITH APPLE

This is a derivative of Pablo Picasso's famous painting, *Boy with a Pipe*. In his painting, the pipe signifies the growing maturity of a young man. My painting depicts a young African American boy holding an apple, which symbolizes life and his determination to live. This speaks to the many unfortunate and untimely deaths of adolescent boys that take place in our country.

48in x 36in
Acrylic Mixed Media on Canvas

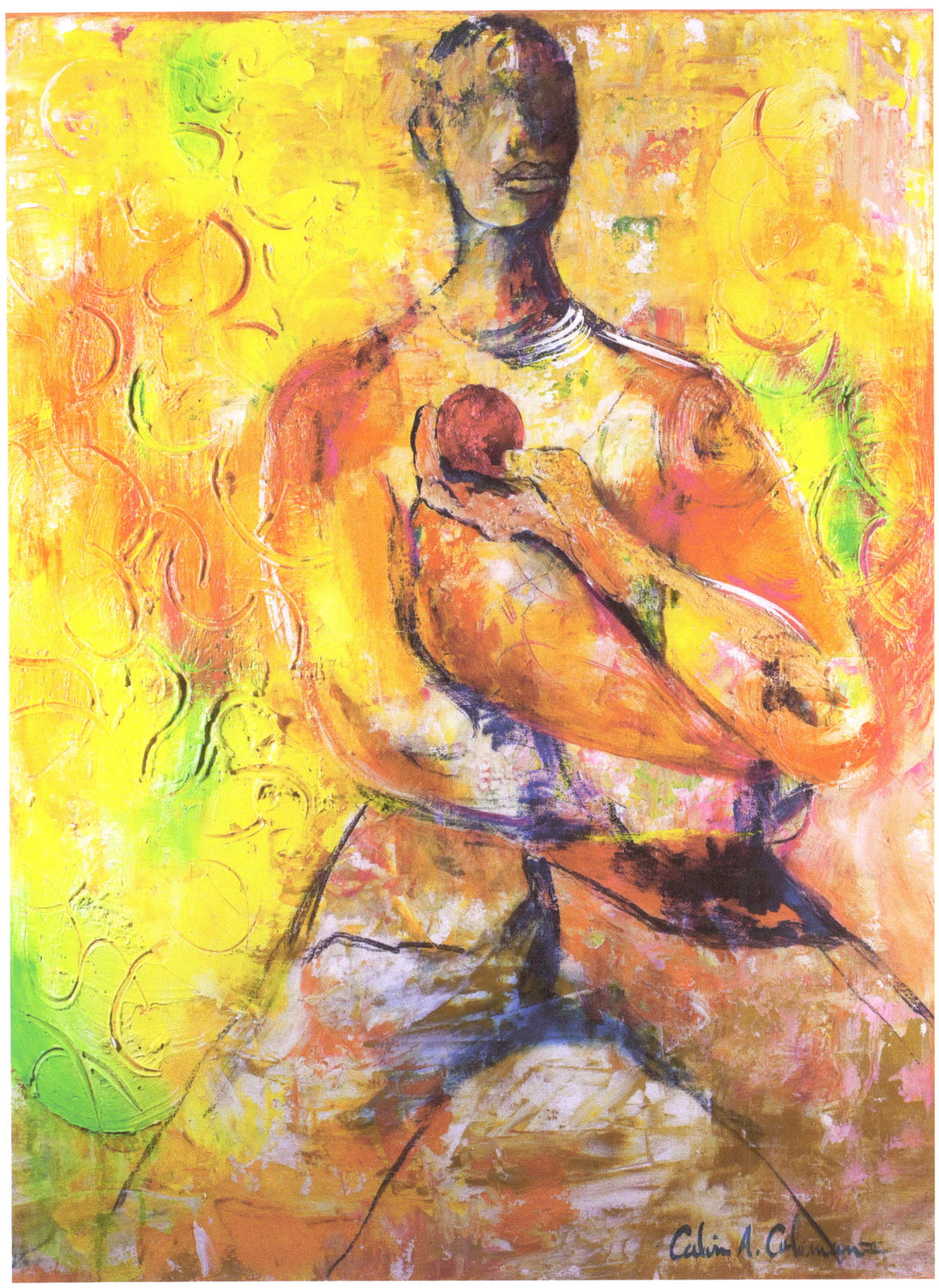

THE THANKFUL FAMILY

A depiction of a family sharing their thankfulness (to God) for a fruitful life. I decided to place the subjects at the far end of the table to give them some depth but to still have them connected to their loved ones. The painting is meant to be subtle, but with a very strong family-centered message.

**This painting currently hangs in the Community of Hope's Family Health and Birth Center in Washington, DC.*

30in x 40in
Acrylic on Canvas

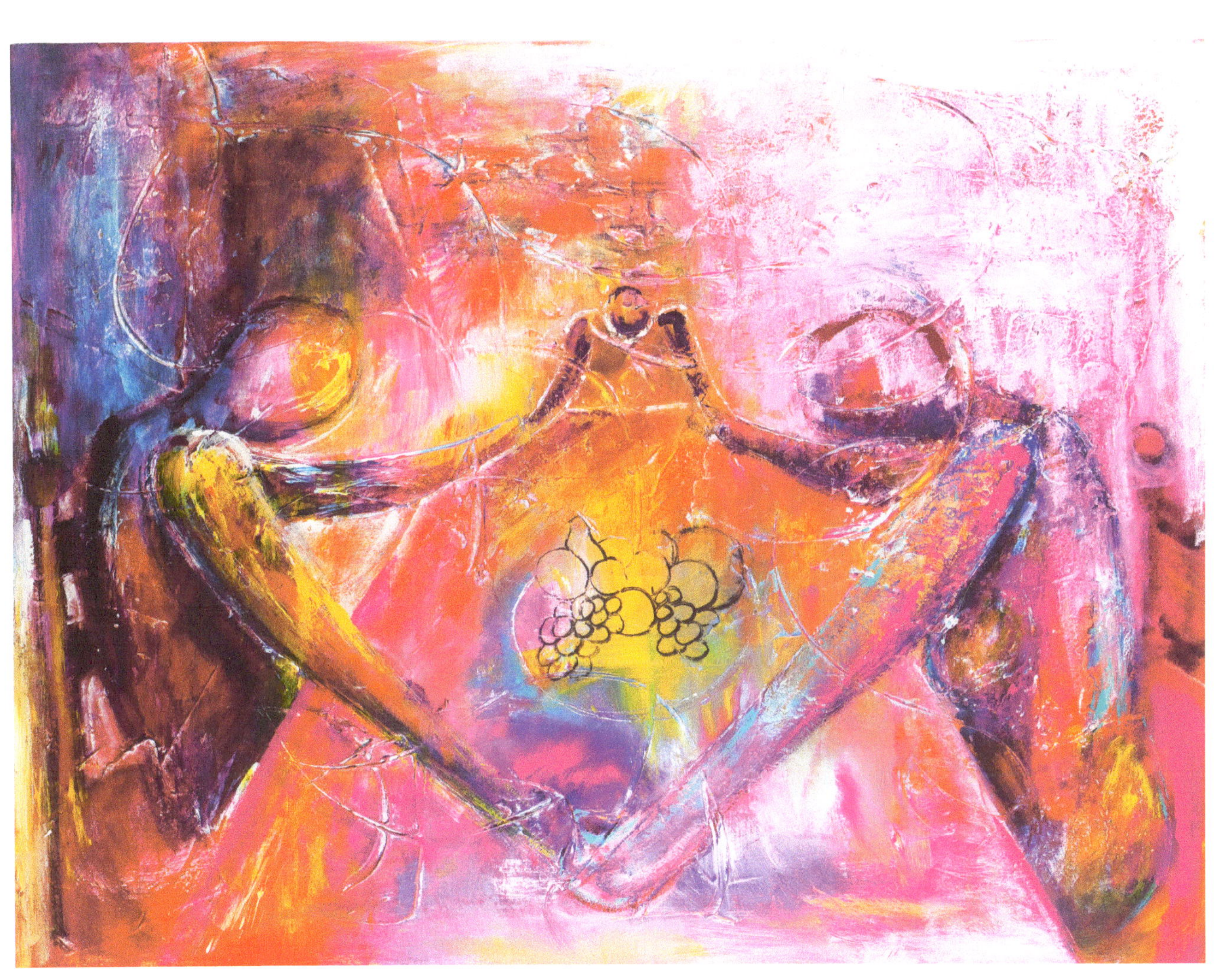

THE RECLINING WOMAN

This painting pays homage to one of my influences, sculptor Henry Moore. In the same vein as Moore, I wanted to paint a full-figured woman that has style and grace. The painting, has a burst of vibrant value and hues that show a woman sitting among flowers in a meadow.

11x14in
Acrylic Mixed Media on Canvas

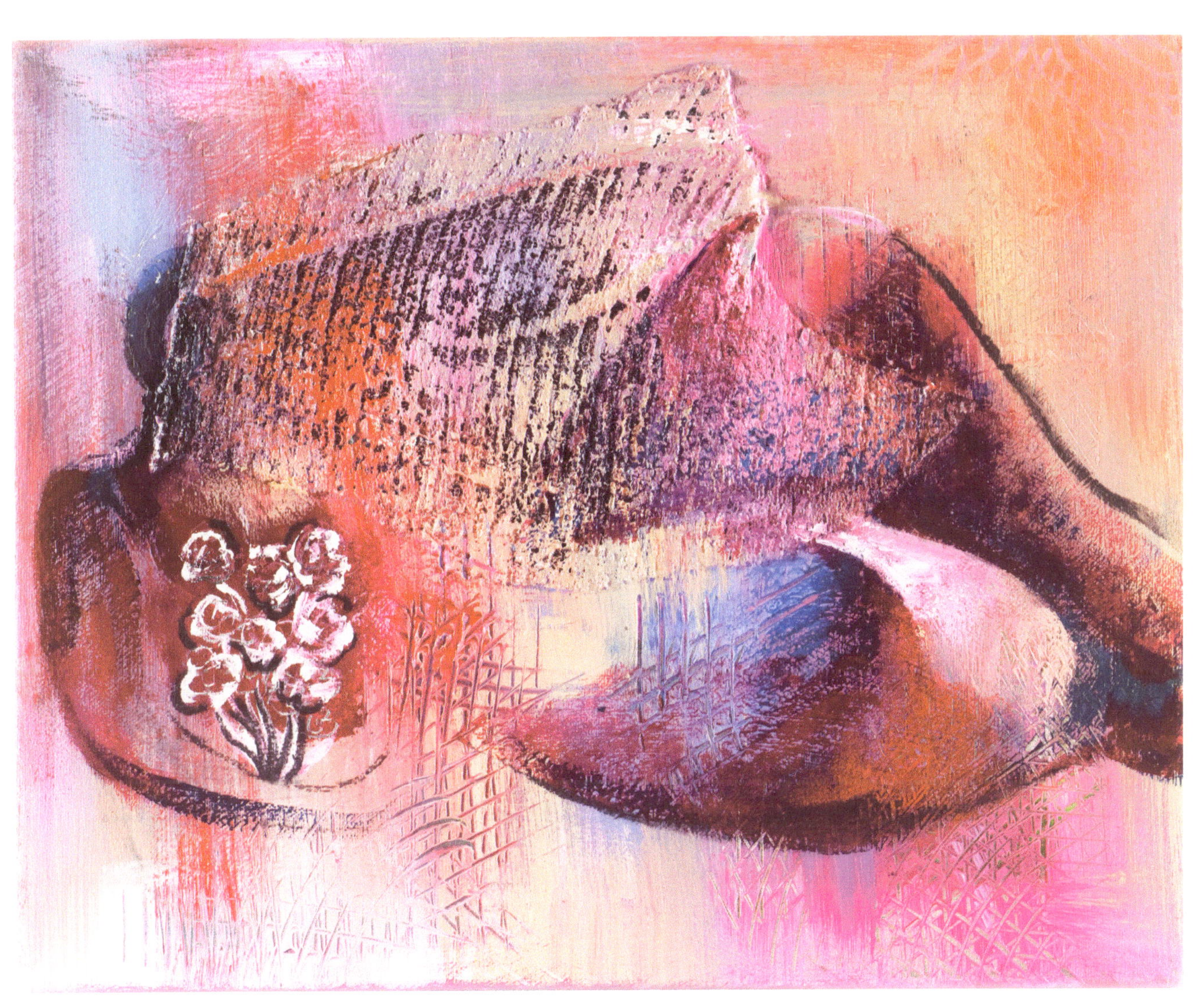

BLUE FLOWERS

Blue Flowers depicts the gracefulness of a woman reclining outdoors. By using a monochromatic style, my goal was to provide the viewer with a greater depth in perception while studying the painting.

36in x 56in
Acrylic Mixed Media on Canvas

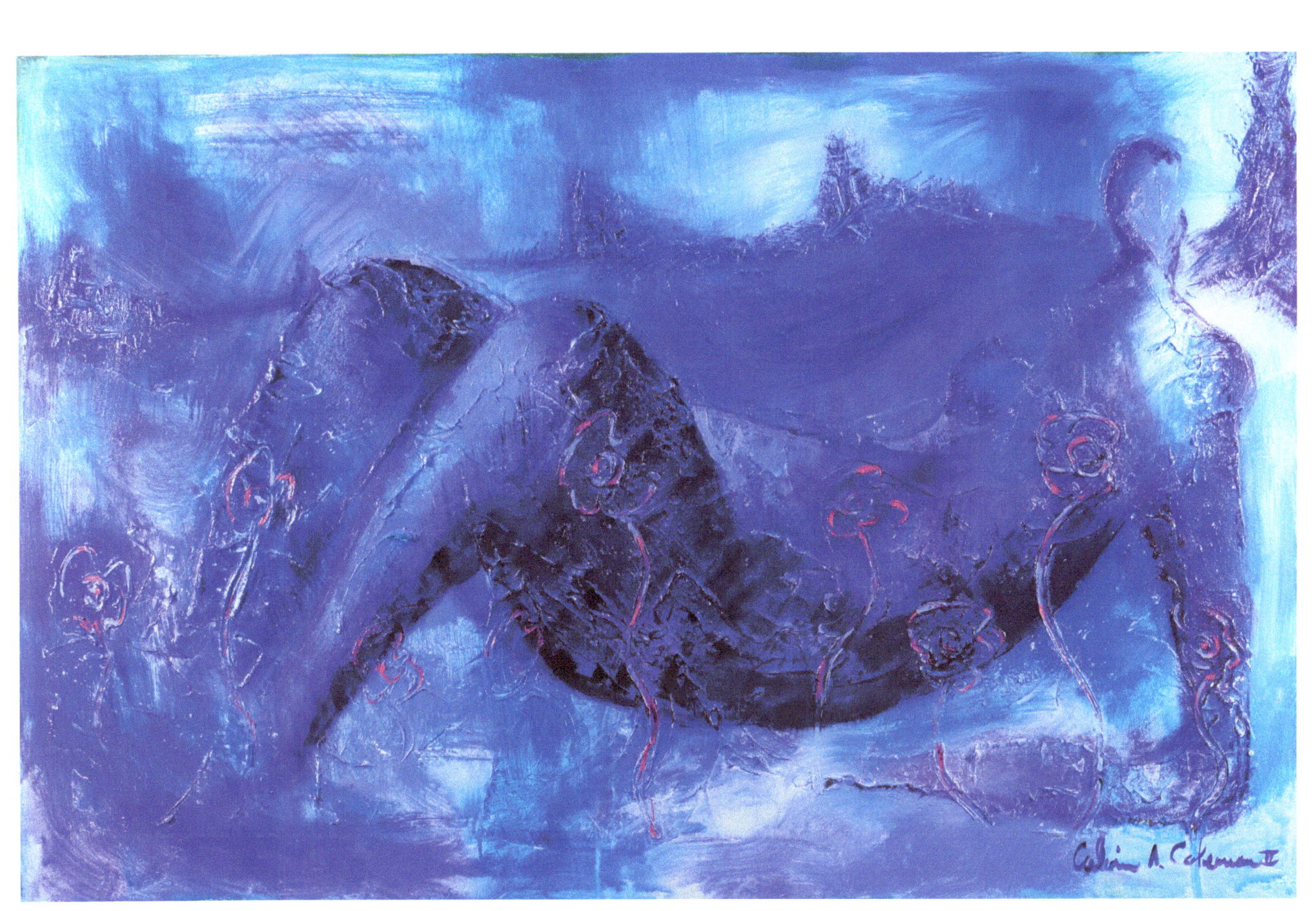

THANKFUL

Thankful was designed to be both ironic and touching. I wanted to have a contrast between the soft colors of blue and aqua (which are typically used to represent sadness) and the image of thankfulness and hope. The result is that all of these emotions coalescece within the painting forcing the viewer to think deeply about what it means to be thankful regardless of what you may have in front of you.

30in x 30in
Acrylic Mixed Media on Canvas

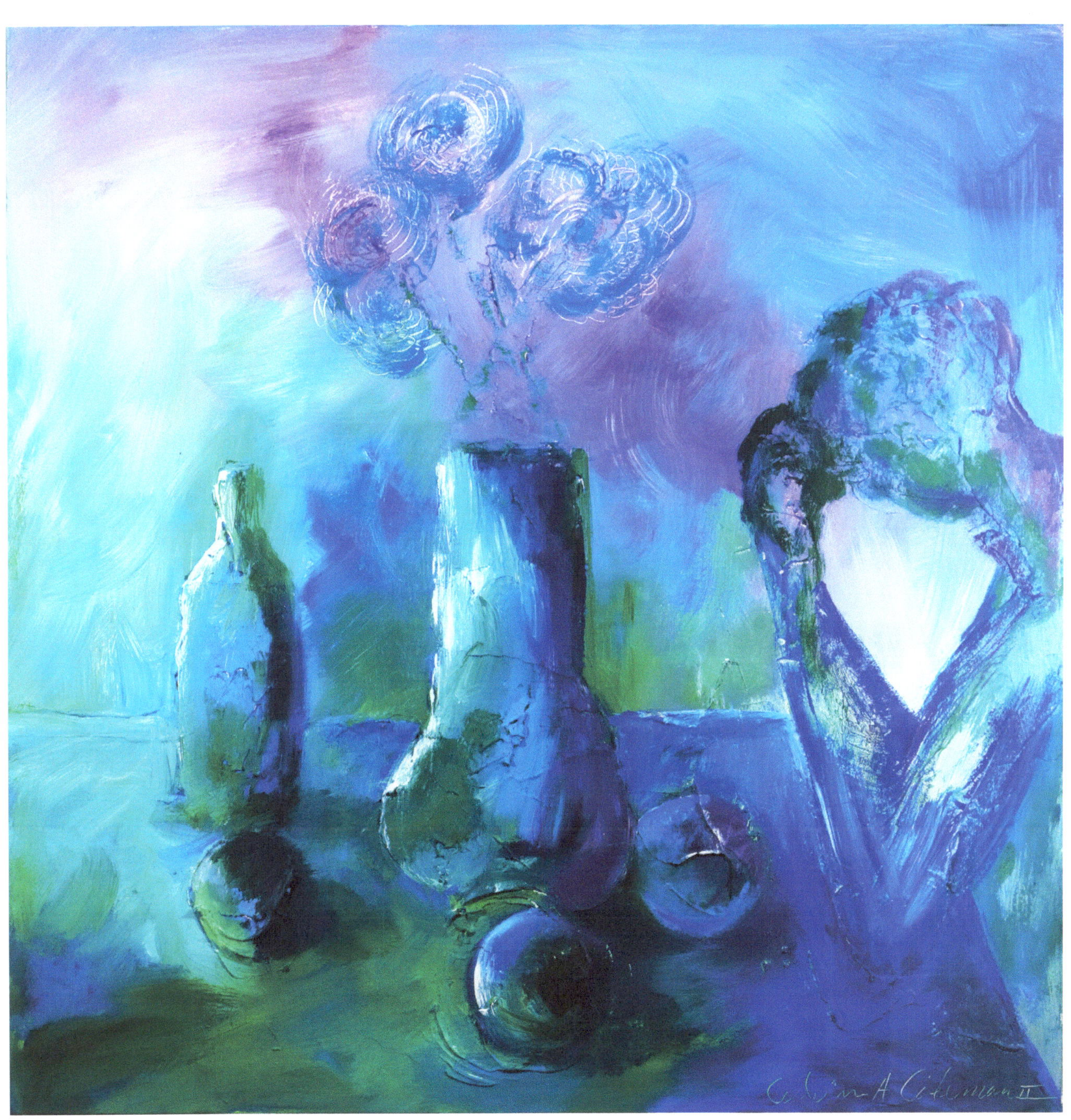

THE RESTING WOMAN

As a painter and an artist, I am heavily influenced by the work of Henri Matisse and I studied and adapted his style of *Fauvism* (the use of many colors). In this painting, I purposely used vibrant colors to allow the subject to "rest" peacefully within the scene.

11in x 14in
Acrylic on Wood

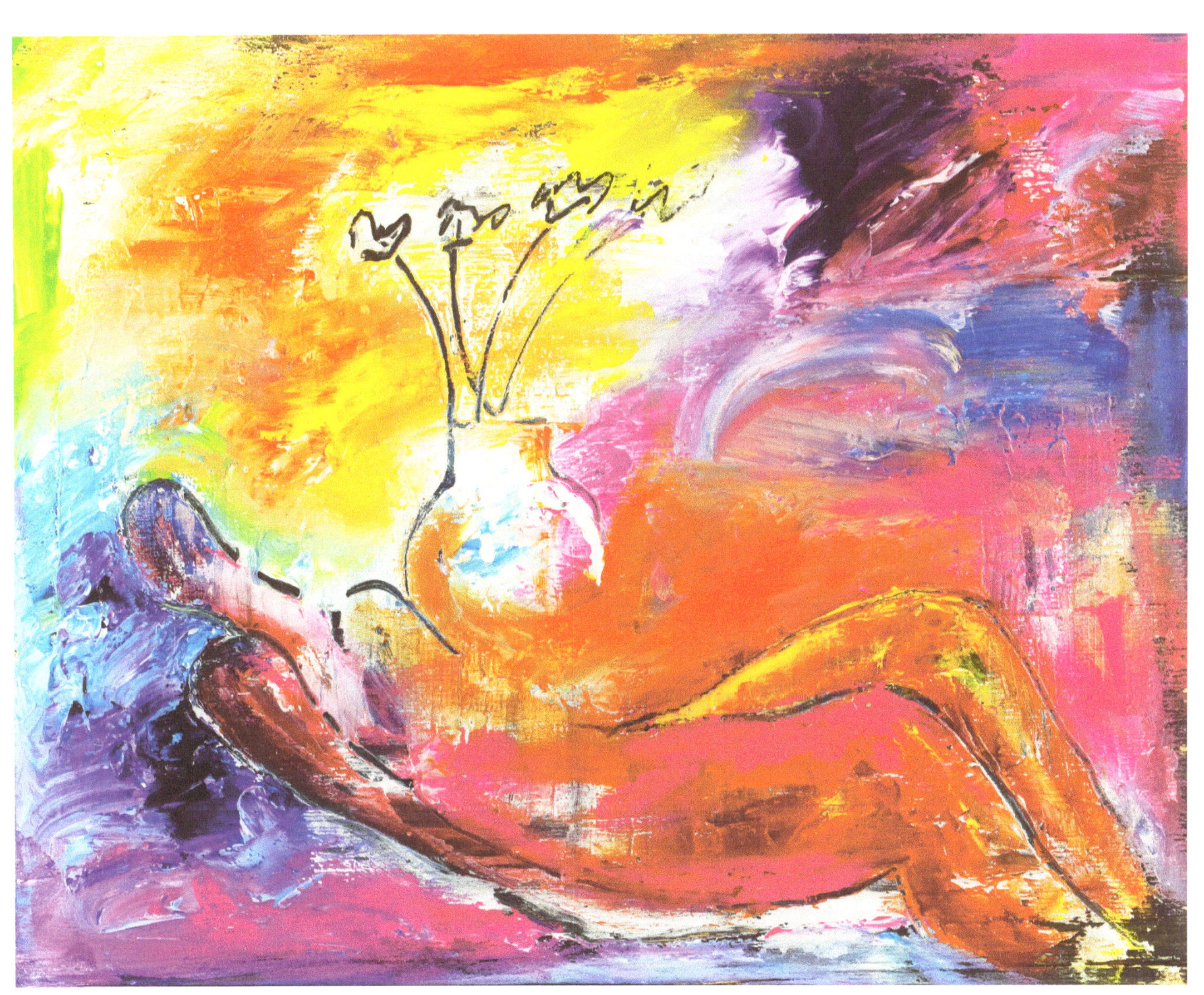

POSTURE

As I continued to study the life of Matisse, I started to experiment with his different styles. The simplistic yet captivating technique that I used in this painting allowed me to create a work of art by using the simple curves and lines in a human's body, cutting them out in such as way to appear as if the figure is in harmony with itself. This collage is one of a few that I created on wood.

11in x 14in
Acrylic Mixed Media on Wood

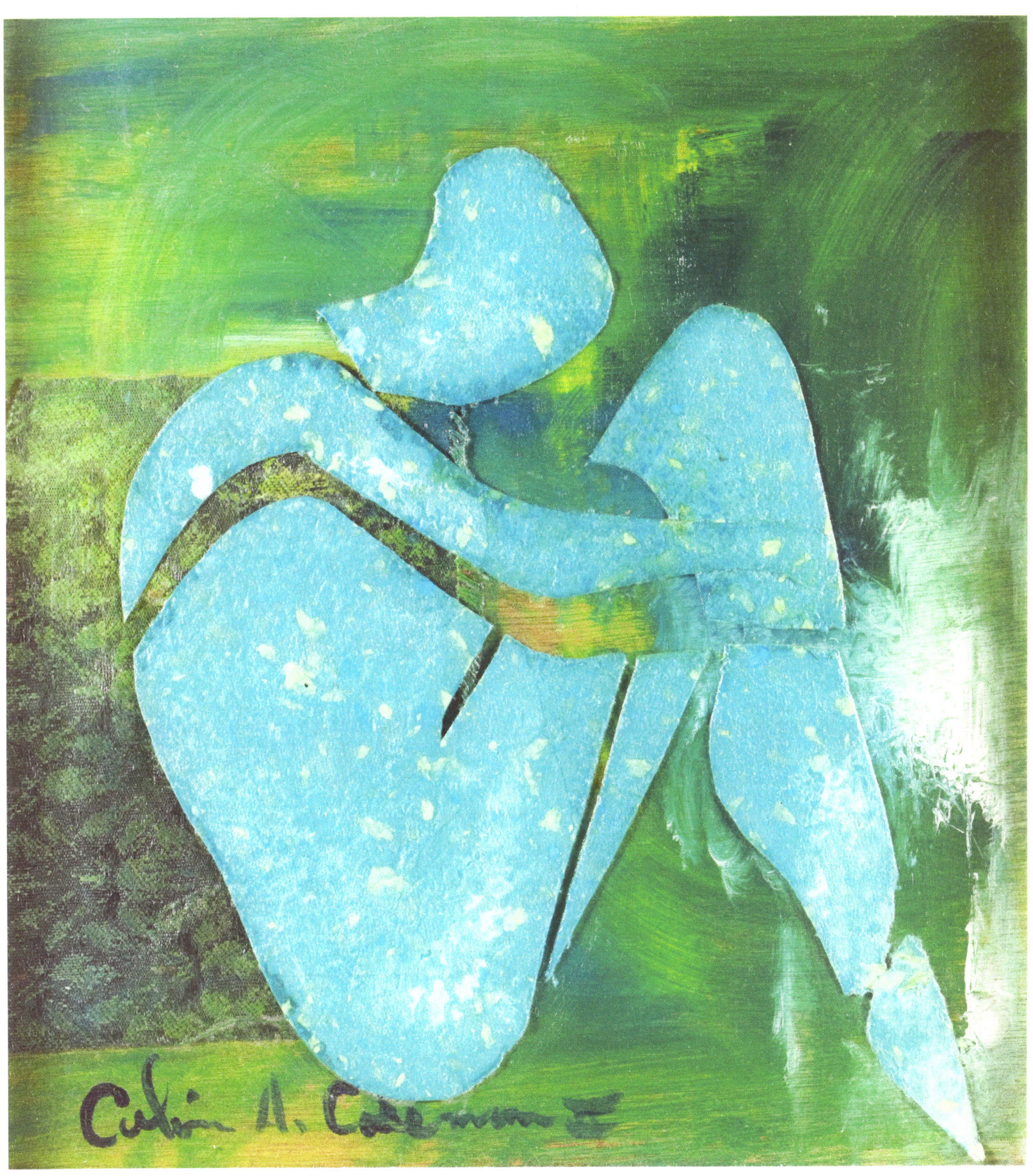

HER PLACID SETTING

One of the things that I enjoy incorporating into my work is the art of simplicity. This painting on wood is of a woman in a lying position. It is generic in shape and in positioning. The stillness of her posture moves me as much as a work that I have created that has great detail. In my world, simplicity is akin to peacefulness.

11x14in
Acrylic on Wood

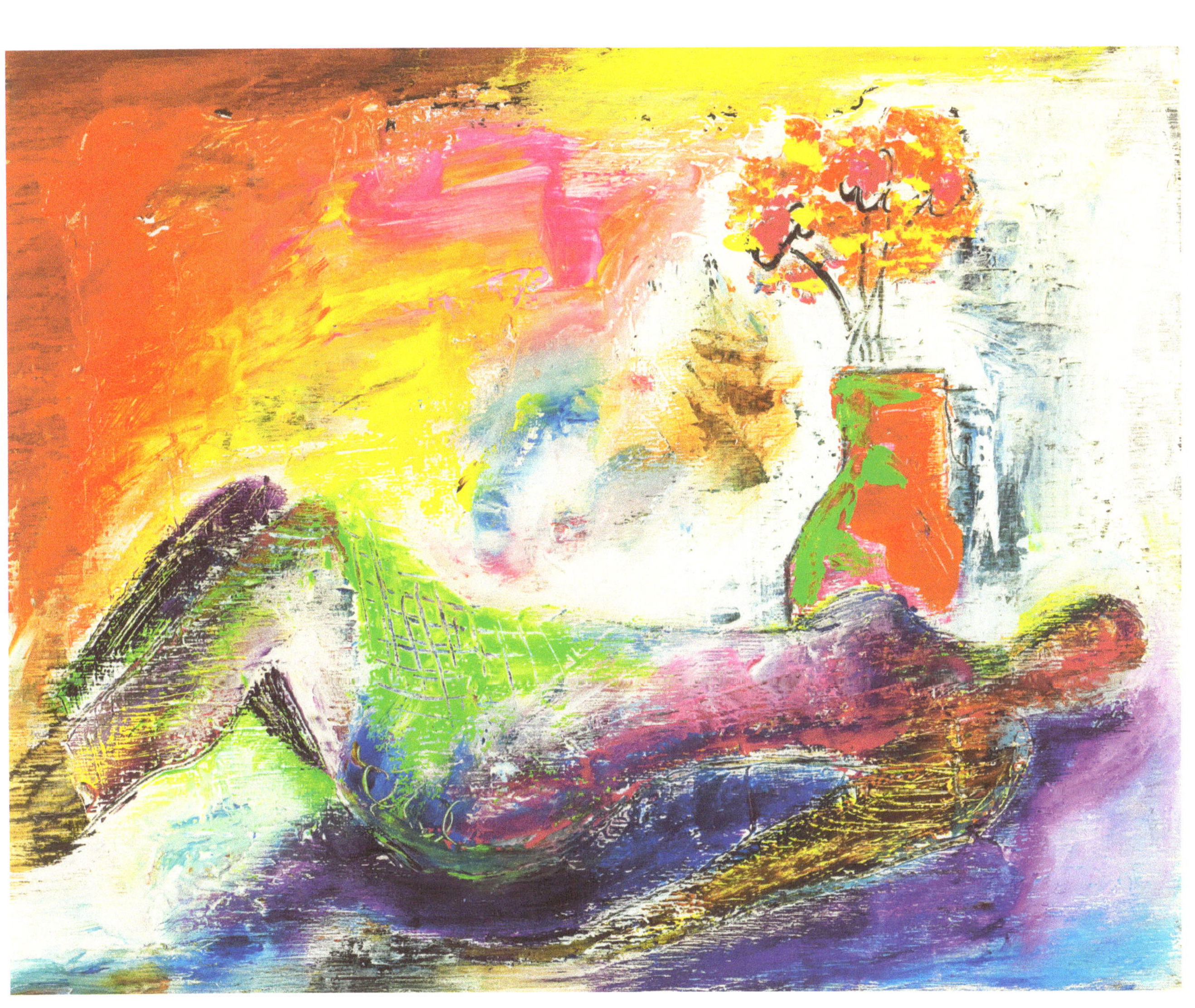

STILL FRUIT

Still fruit paintings are dear to me because they keep me grounded and connected to the technical part of painting and sketching (which includes perception and placement of objects) and they allow me to use a whimsical approach to painting. This is a standard setting of a still life, yet it offers a nonstandard painting technique.

12in x 12in x 1in
Acrylic on Wood

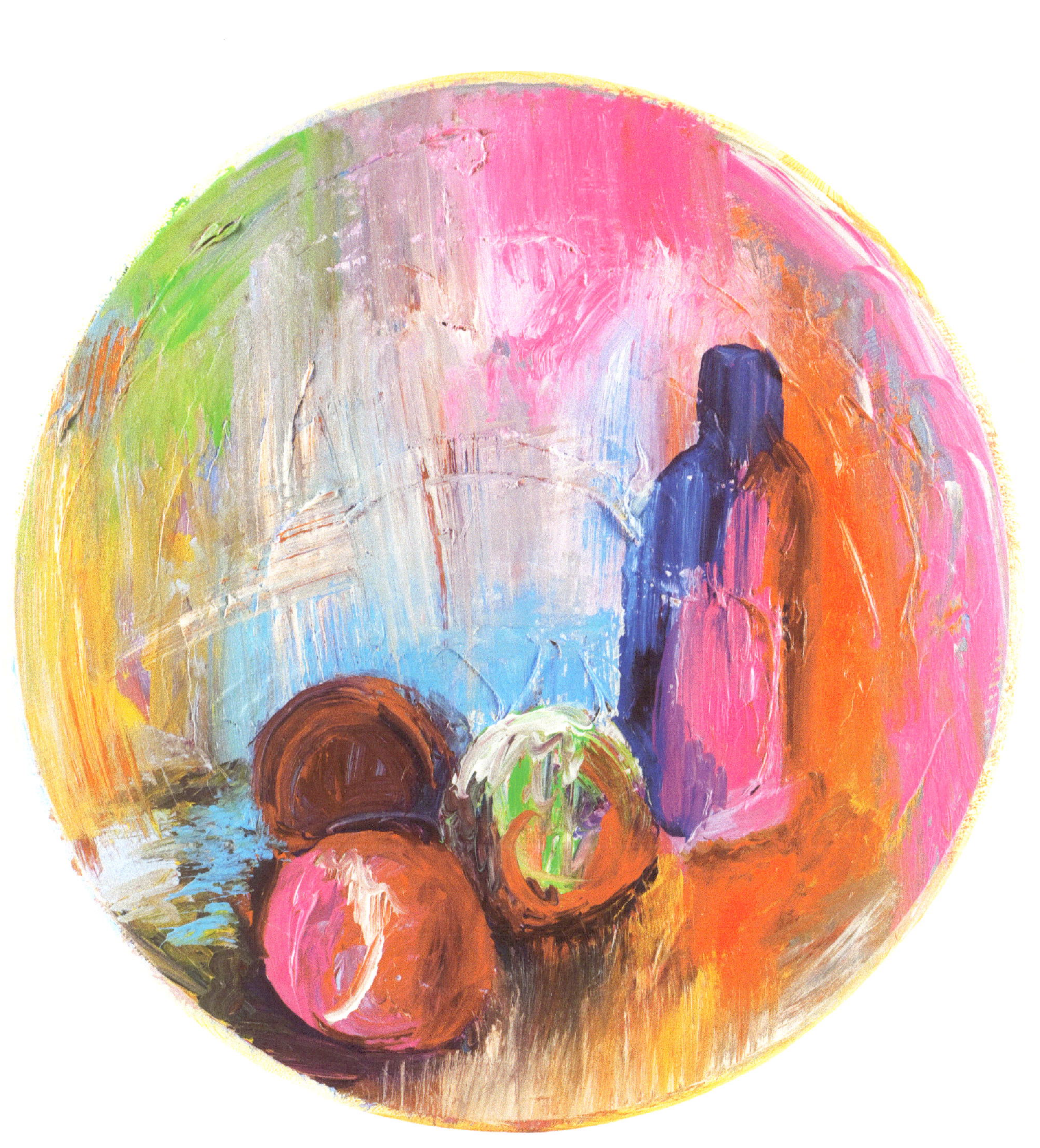

IN PURPLE

In Purple captures the dark shadows of the subjects with a deep purple and contrasts them with a light from the lightest color visible. The result is a painting that is both subtle and bold. This is one of the few paintings that I have created using a watercolor technique.

20in x 16in
Acrylic on Canvas

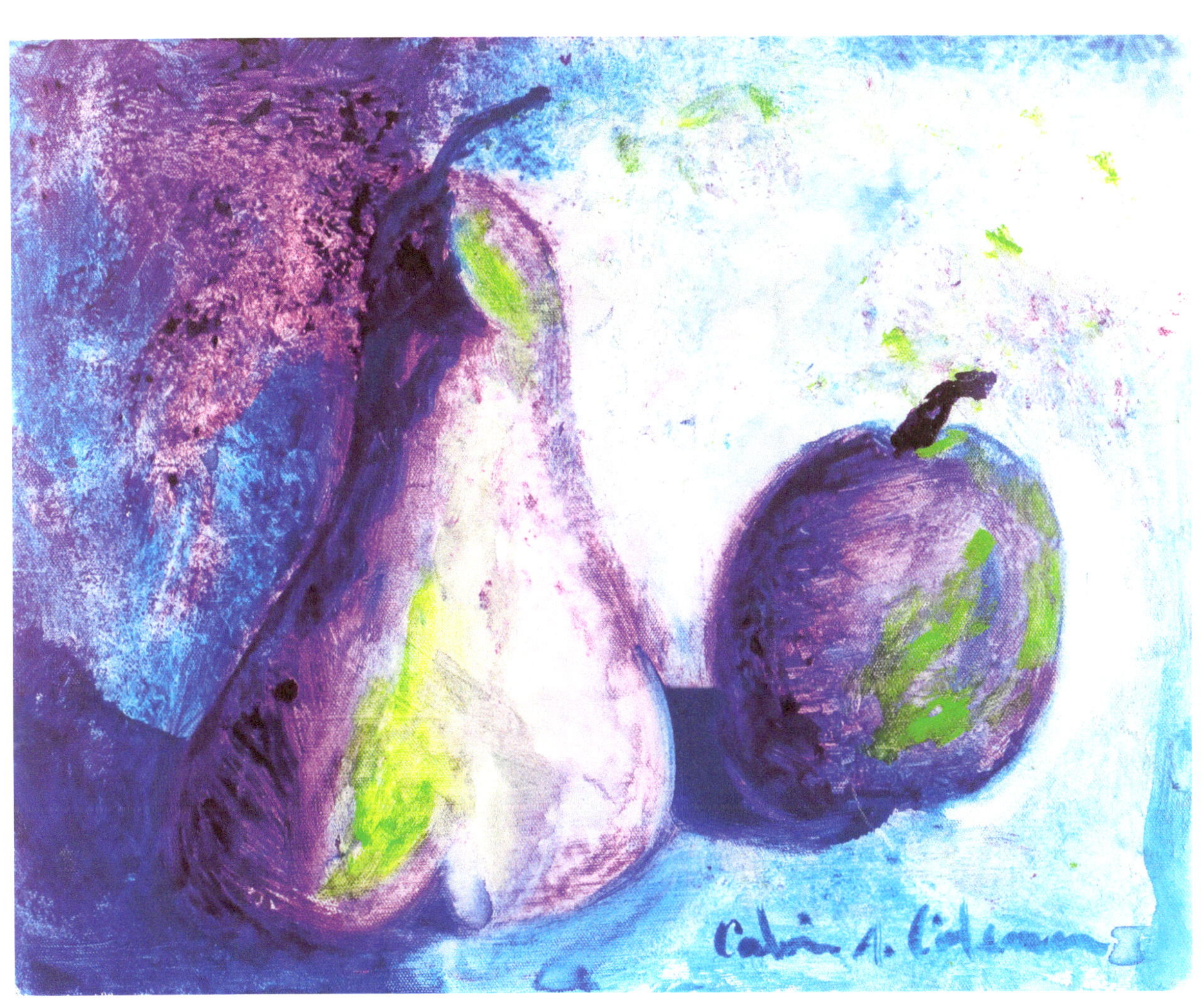

THE TEXTURED WOMAN

As a painter, one of my goals is to be uninhibited when I am creating, which allows me to experiment with a myriad of carving tools, compounds, textiles and surfaces. In this painting, to break the monotony of a particular painted texture, I used a sculpting tool to create a patterned scratching imprint in her dress.

36in x 42in
Acrylic Mixed Media on Canvas

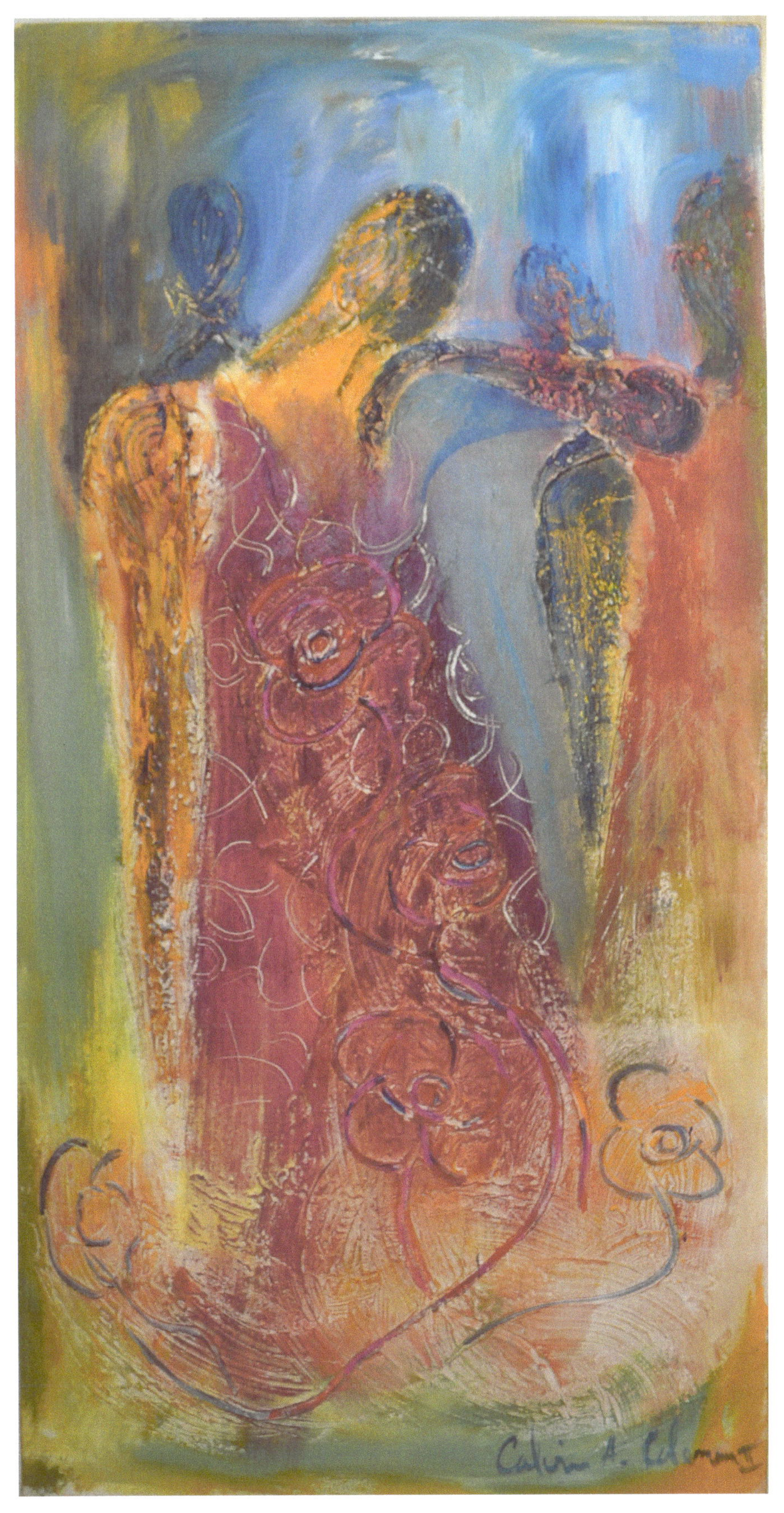

SIMPLICITY

The process of using various techniques and combining them with various influences is important to me. This multimedia collage embodies the influence of Henry Moore and Henri Matisse, which includes the technical process of cutting out material to create your subject in simple form.

11in x 14in
Acrylic Mixed Media on Canvas

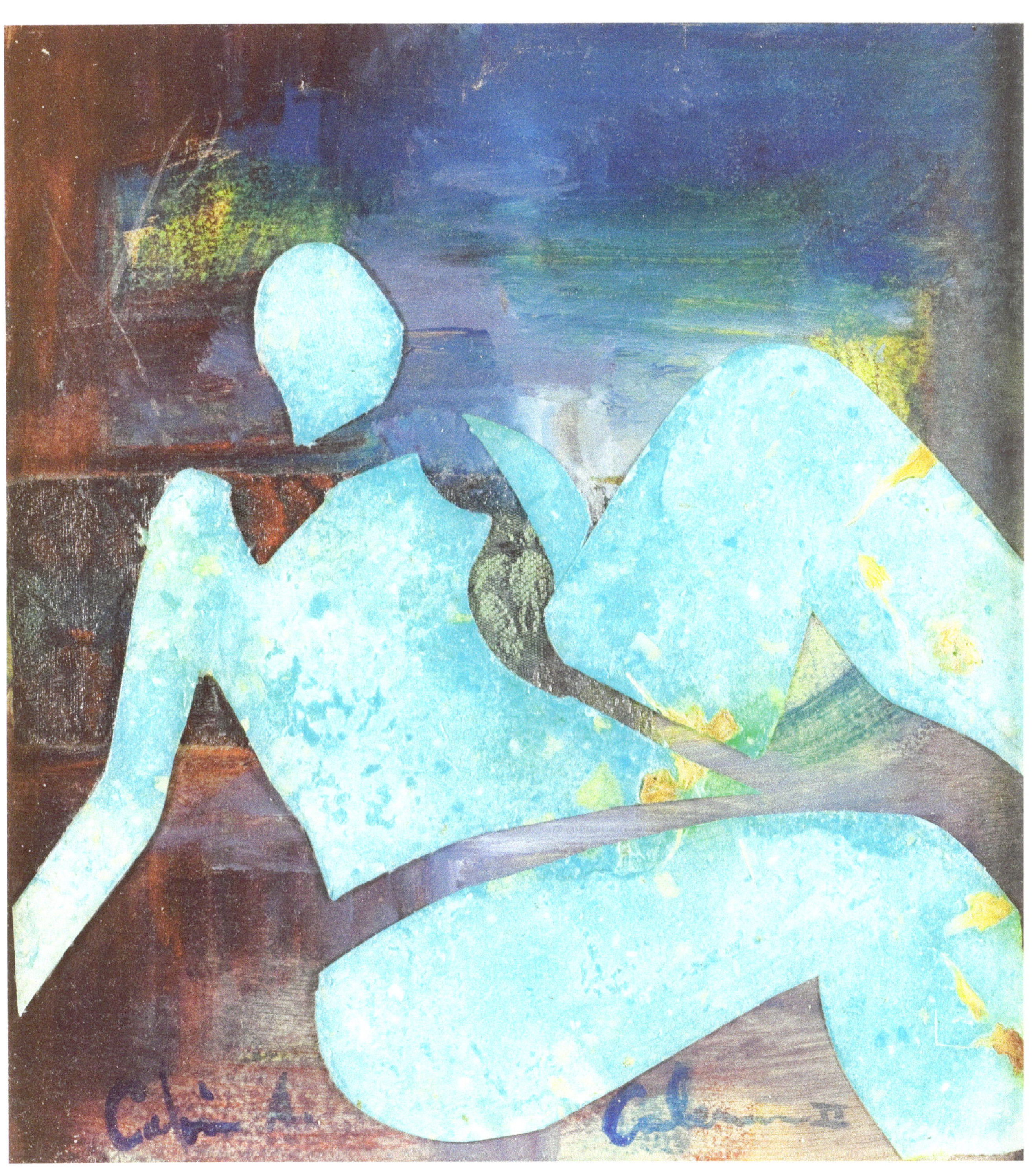

RECIPE IN COLORS

This painting reflects a watercolor technique with the use of acrylic paint and applied water. I often apply water with a spray applicator that allows the paint to sit in puddles and dilutes the various hues into a multitude of values. I use it to create my own version of tie dyed art on the canvas.

20in x 16in
Acrylic on Canvas

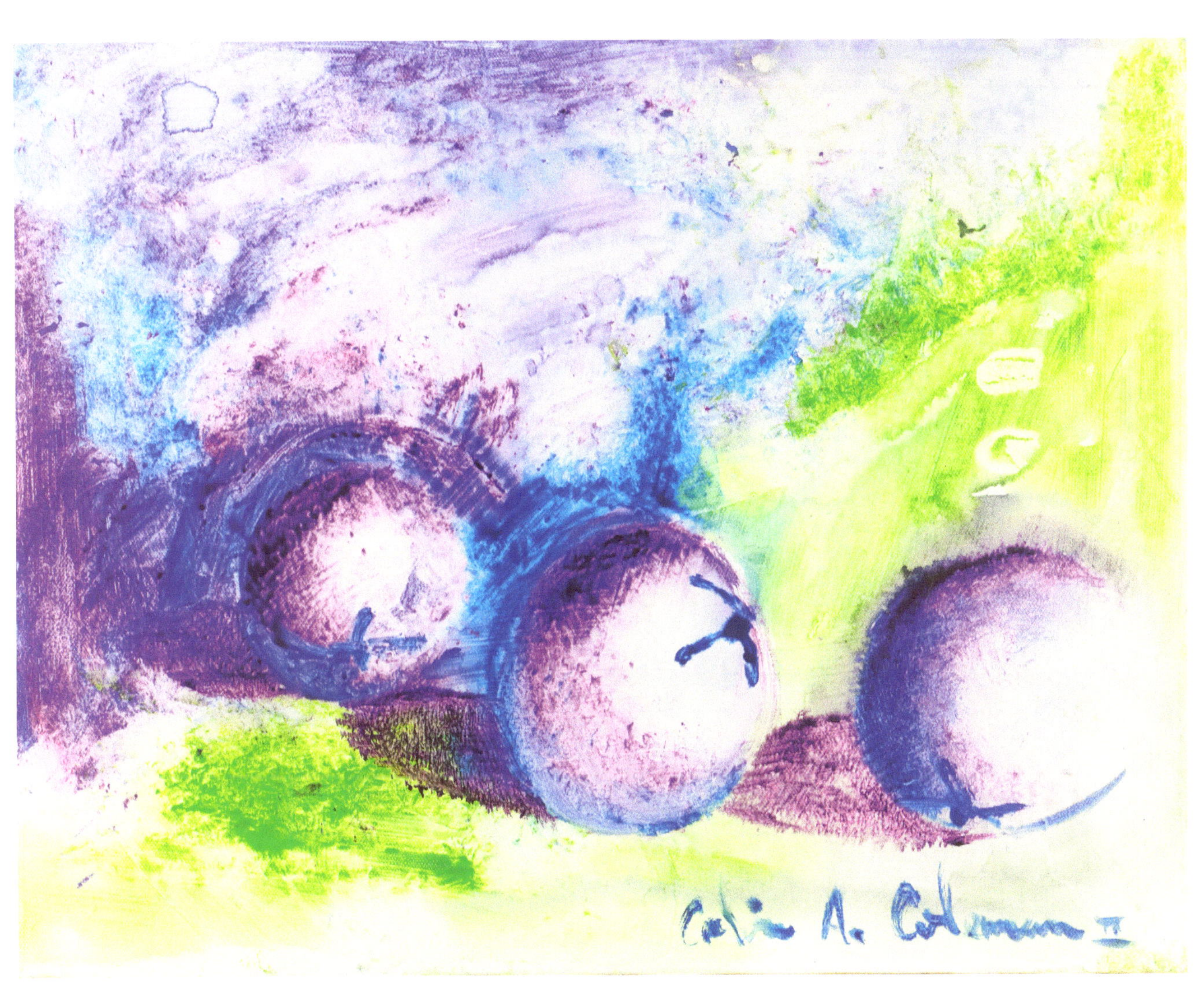

MOMENT OF SERENITY

Sometimes I blindly choose my colors for a painting. This is a fun initiative that I started working with in an effort to push my creativity. This painting of a woman is situated very similar to a Fauvist style, with color that invite the viewer to appreciate her serenity. The painting is abstract so that the viewer can see the subject as if she is on the floor, or couch, or somewhere else.

36in x 48in
Acrylic Mixed Media on Canvas

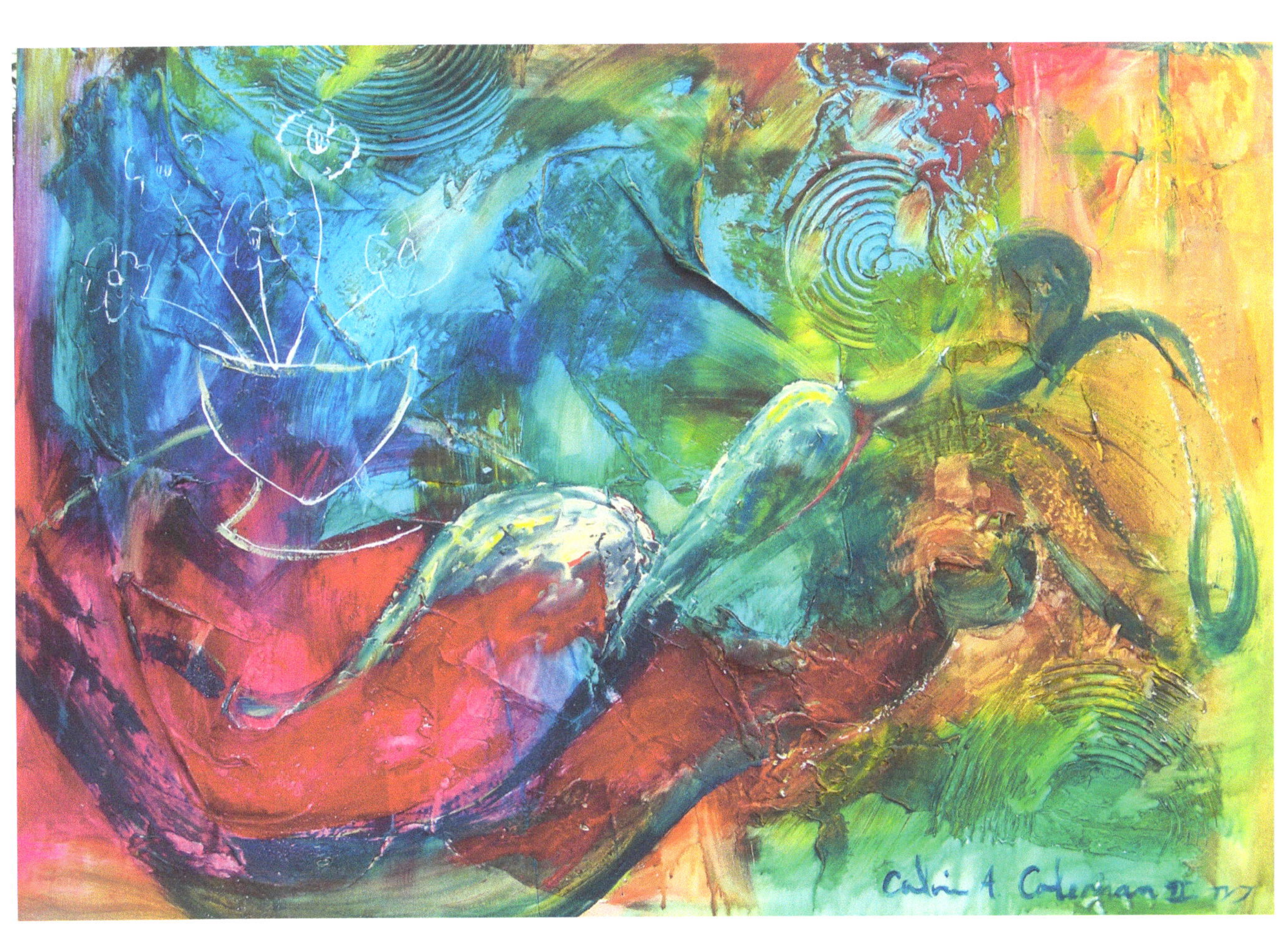

THE GATHERING

This painting was originally featured in the Arts in Embassy Program hosted by the U.S Embassy of Rome, Italy. It depicts a woman that has gathered fruit in her bag and is sitting with them. It was created using an assemblage of paint, collage, and compound paste. It is one of my favorites and is designed to demonstrate the strength and beauty of a woman regardless of her position or title.

40in x 30in
Acrylic Mixed Media on Canvas

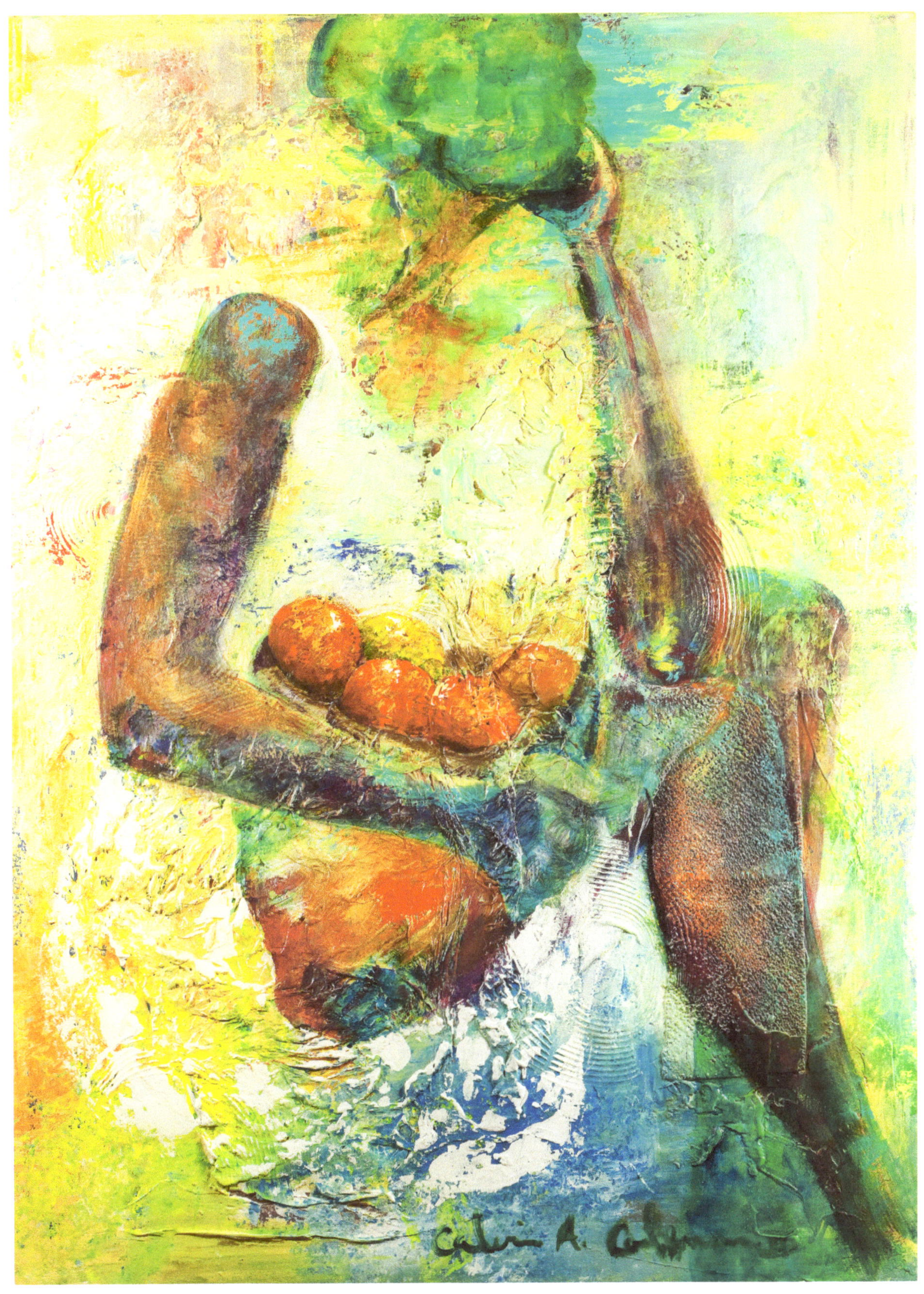

STUDY PAINTING #20CC

Often times, I create a pre-painting that I use before I create the actual painting. This process allows me to try a series of techniques before I create the actual painting on canvas in a larger scale. There are times that the pre sample paintings, in my opinion, turn out better than the larger sized originals.

8in x 10in
Acrylic Mixed Media on Canvas

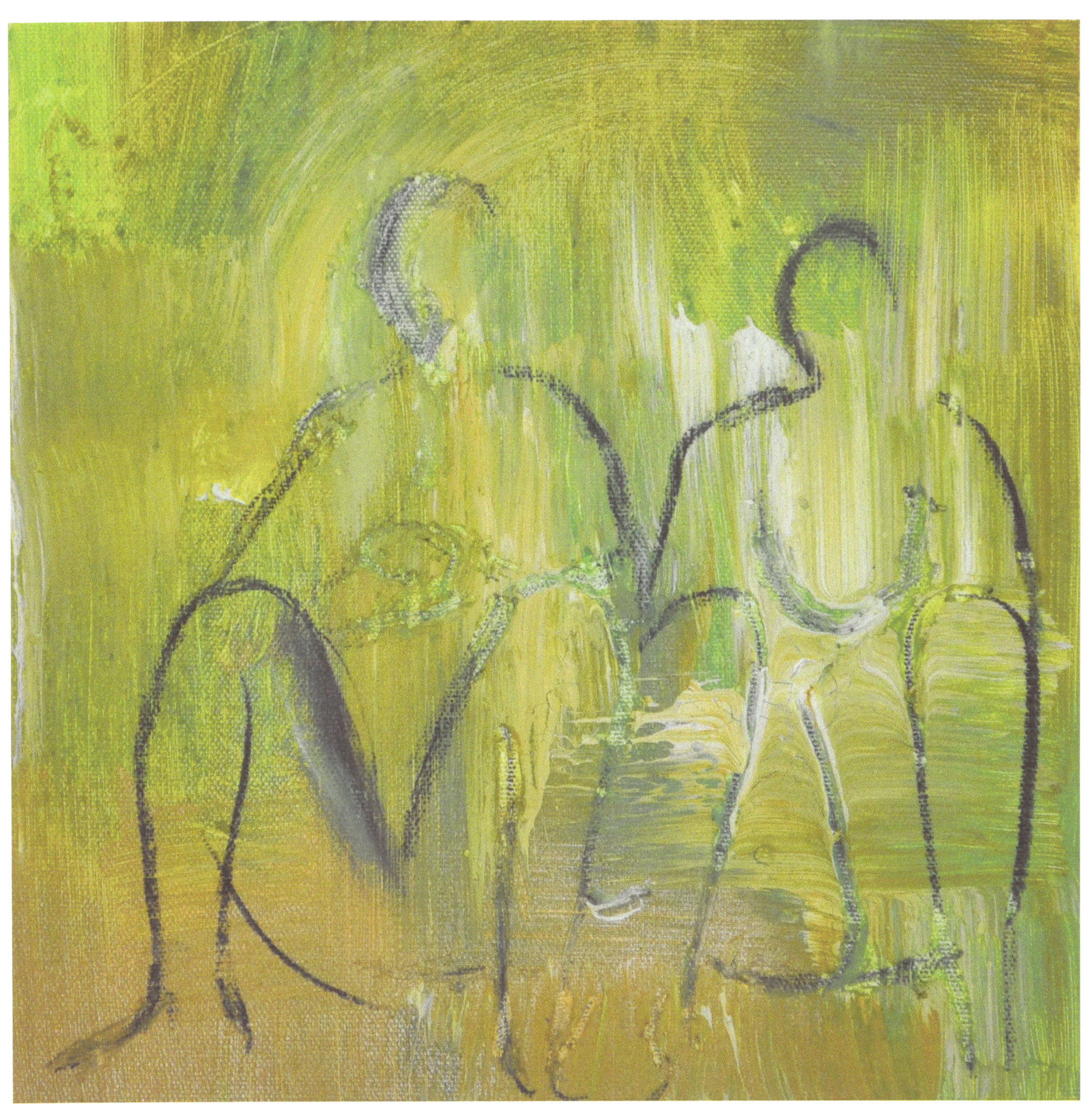

FRUIT AMONG CUBISM

In this painting, I worked hard to stretch my creativity and depict still life in a subtle cubism manner. I have studied the work of Pablo Picasso throughout the years and I have found myself completely engrossed in the way he approached various genres in art. He was definitely an innovator in the world of art and I appreciated his open mindedness and the art that he left for the world.

10in x 10in
Acrylic Mixed Media on Canvas

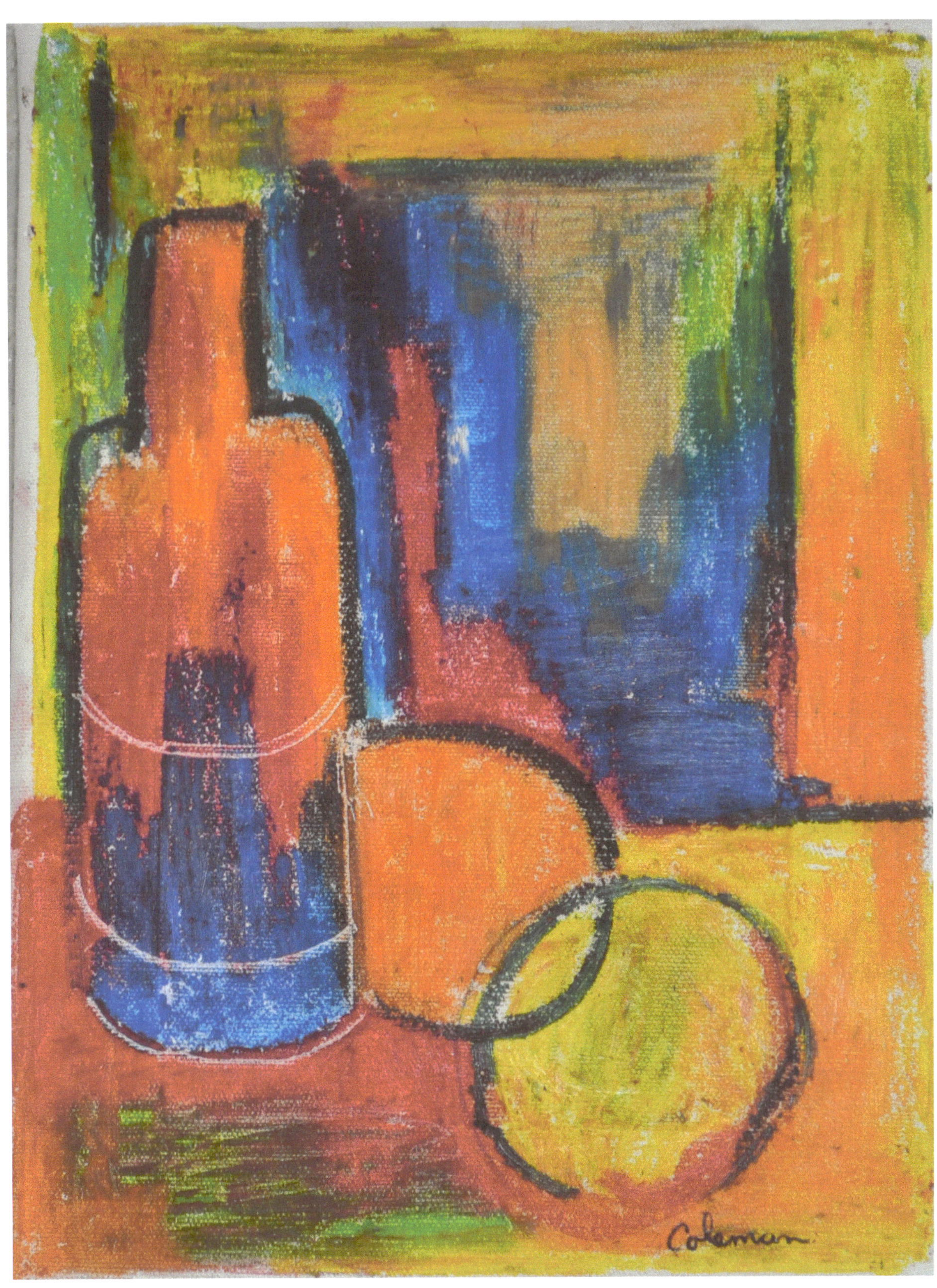
Coleman

AFTER WORK

This painting of a woman in monochromatic blue, reclining on a sofa is meant to be simple in nature and subtle to the eye. This painting depicts a woman after a long day, catching a moment for herself.

10in x 10in
Acrylic on Canvas

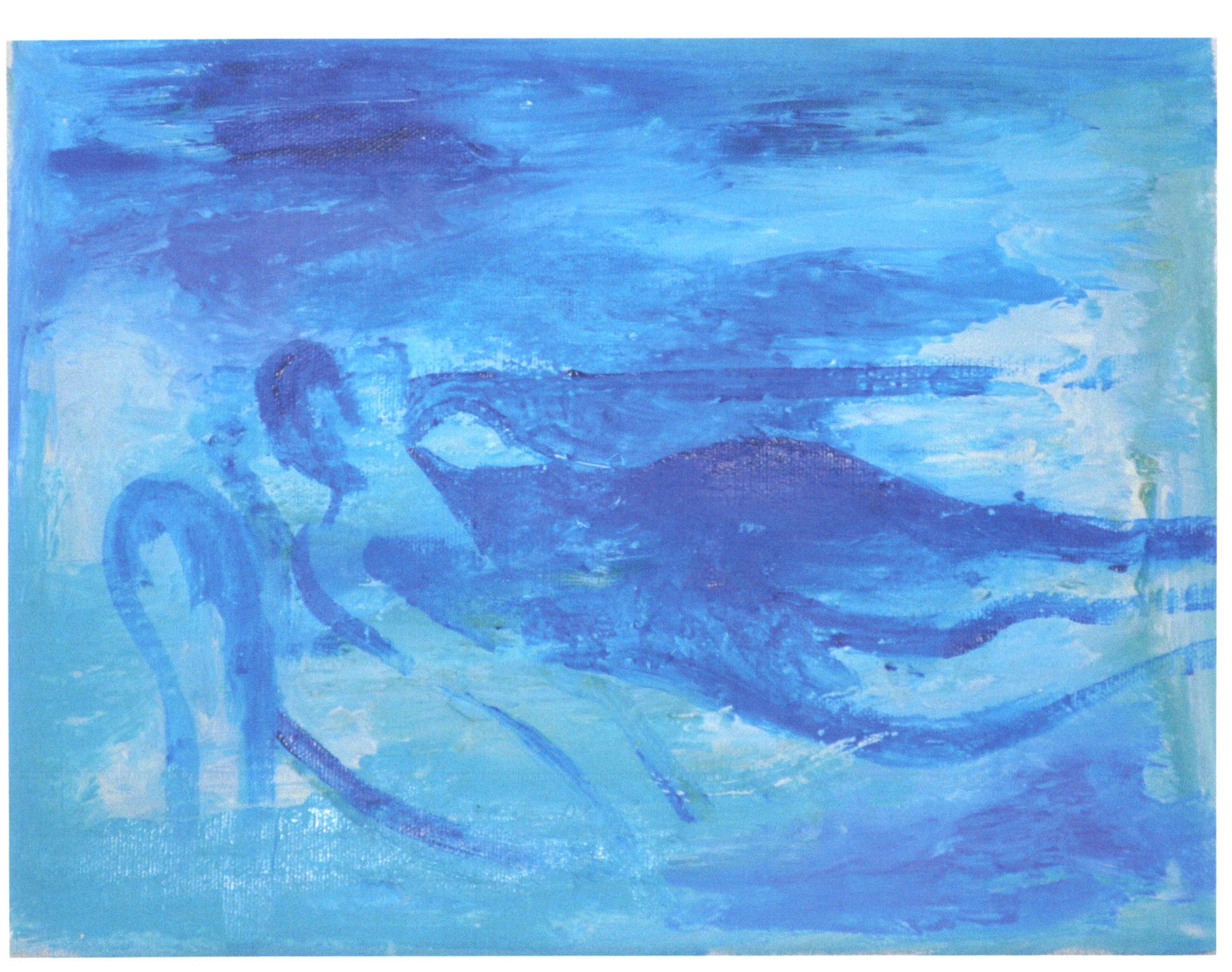

THE COMPOSITION

In this painting, I tried to depict the characteristics of a still life with a small sample of cubism. My process of adding certain characteristics of cubism allows me to visualize the objects in a setting in various perspectives and add them as one.

8in x 10in
Acrylic on Canvas

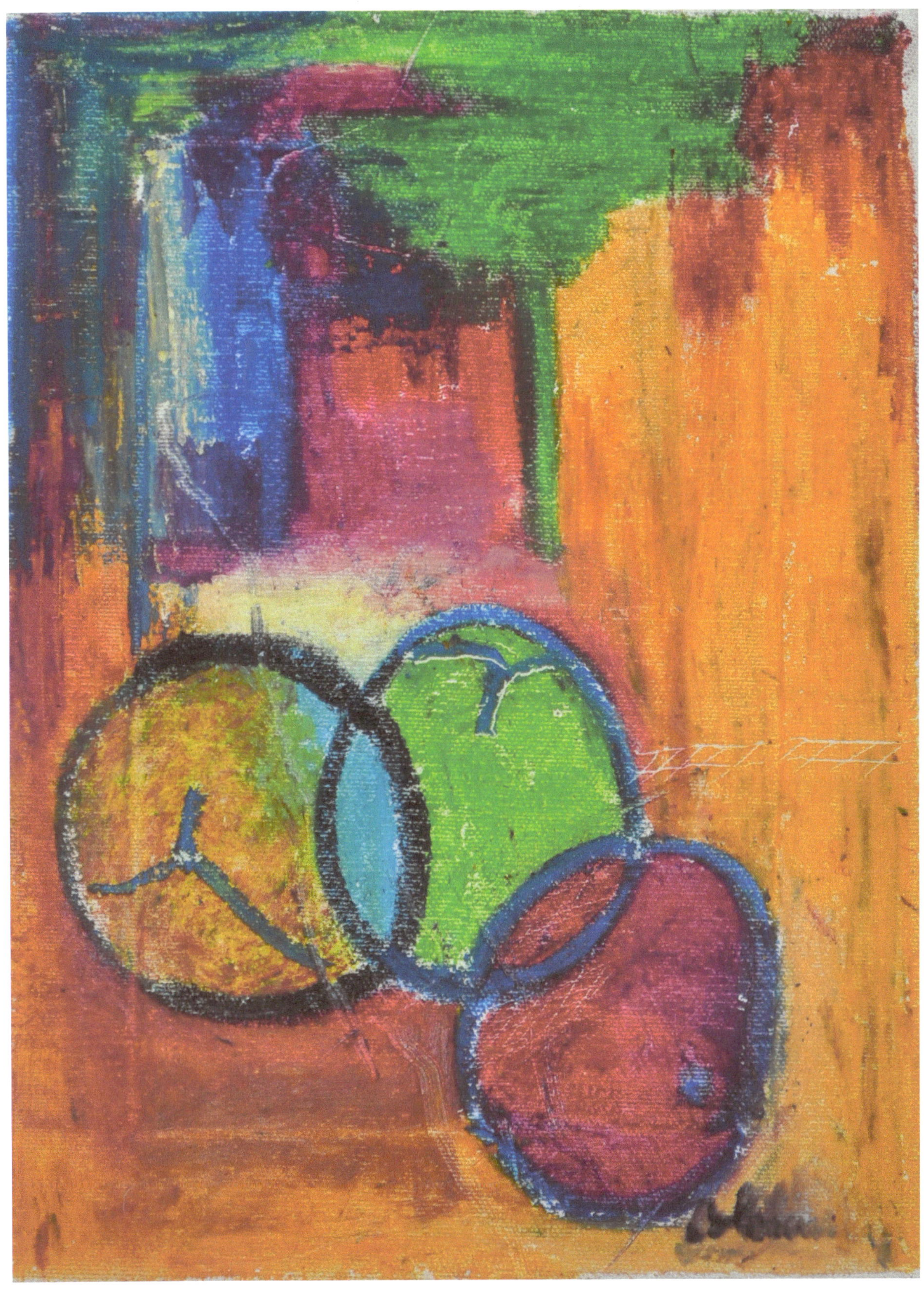

THE SITTING OF A MAN

One of the techniques that can be found in many of my paintings is my use of a variety of colors that are consumed by the subject within the painting. This sitting subject is made up of a number of colors, which, I believe, allows the subject to transcend ethnicity, and barriers.

40in x 30in
Acrylic Mixed Media on Canvas

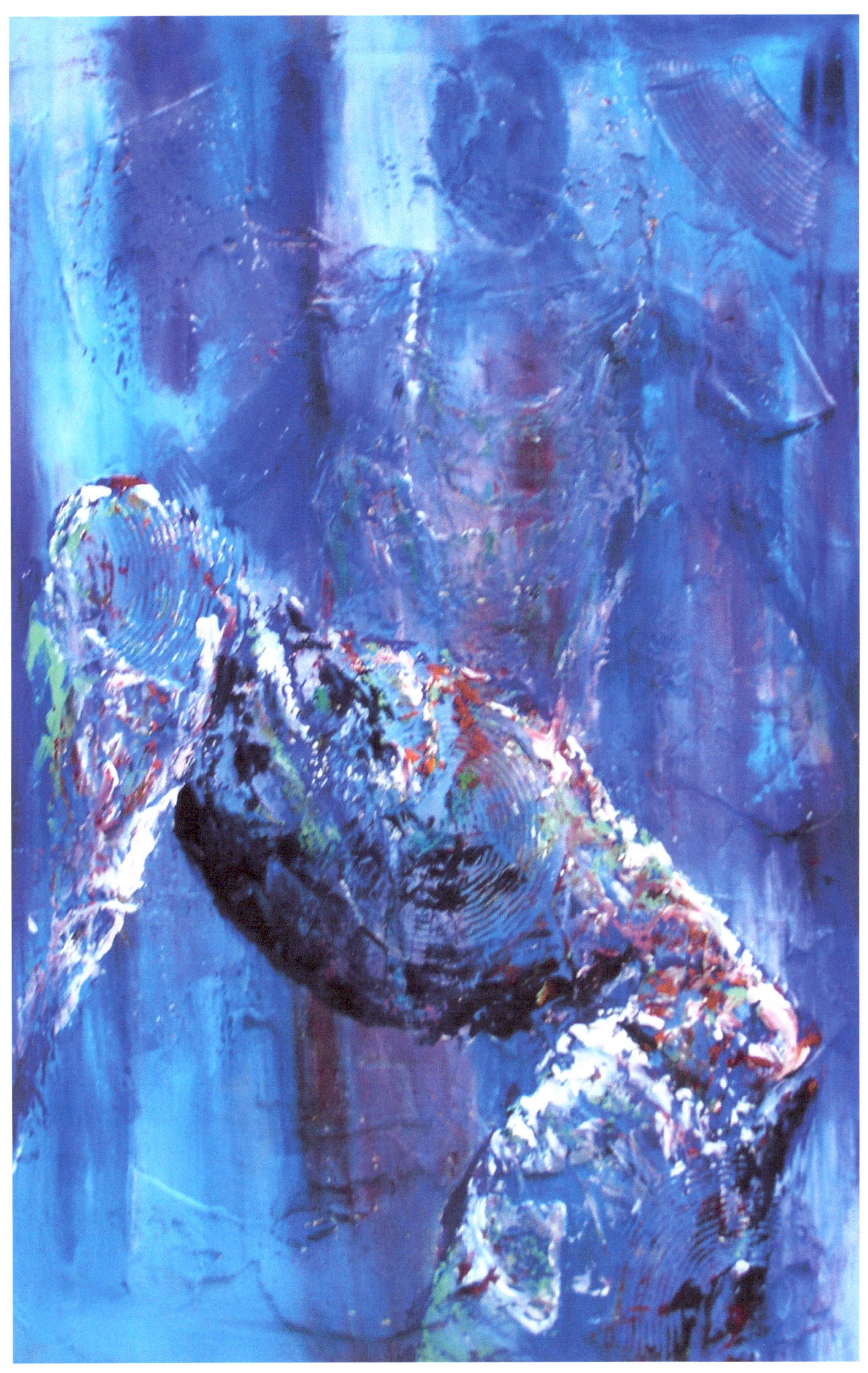

POSITIONED TO CONNECT

This is a painting that is designed to show the closeness and unity of the women based upon the way they are positioned in the painting. Even though they are not holding hands or embracing one another, they are connected.

40in x 30in
Acrylic on Canvas

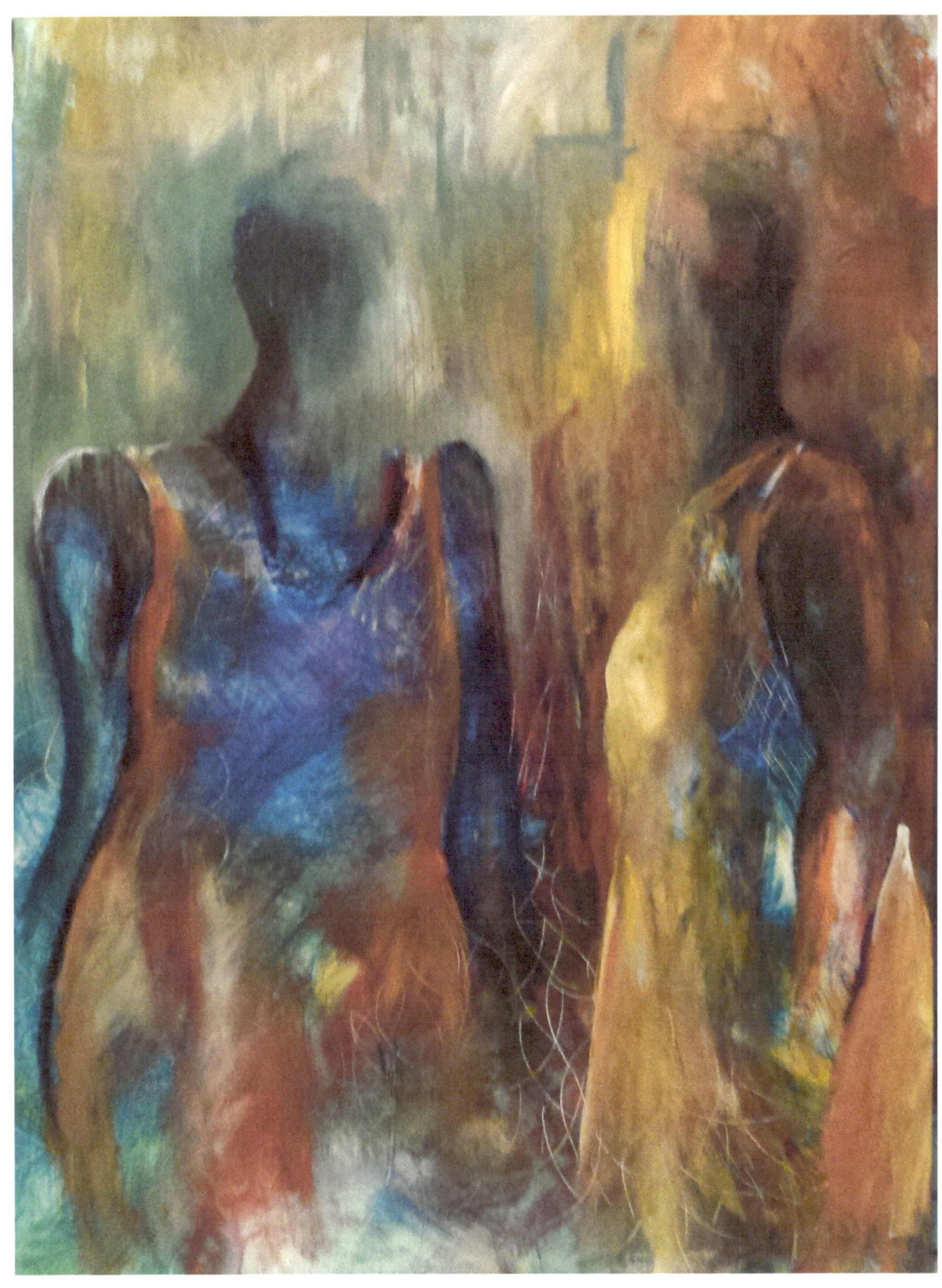

CONNECTION

This painting was created to show the relationship, friendship, and sisterhood between two women. The genre of personal connections among humanity, has offered many images that exhibit just that. One can often read body language and feel the connection between two people.

40in x 30in
Acrylic on Canvas

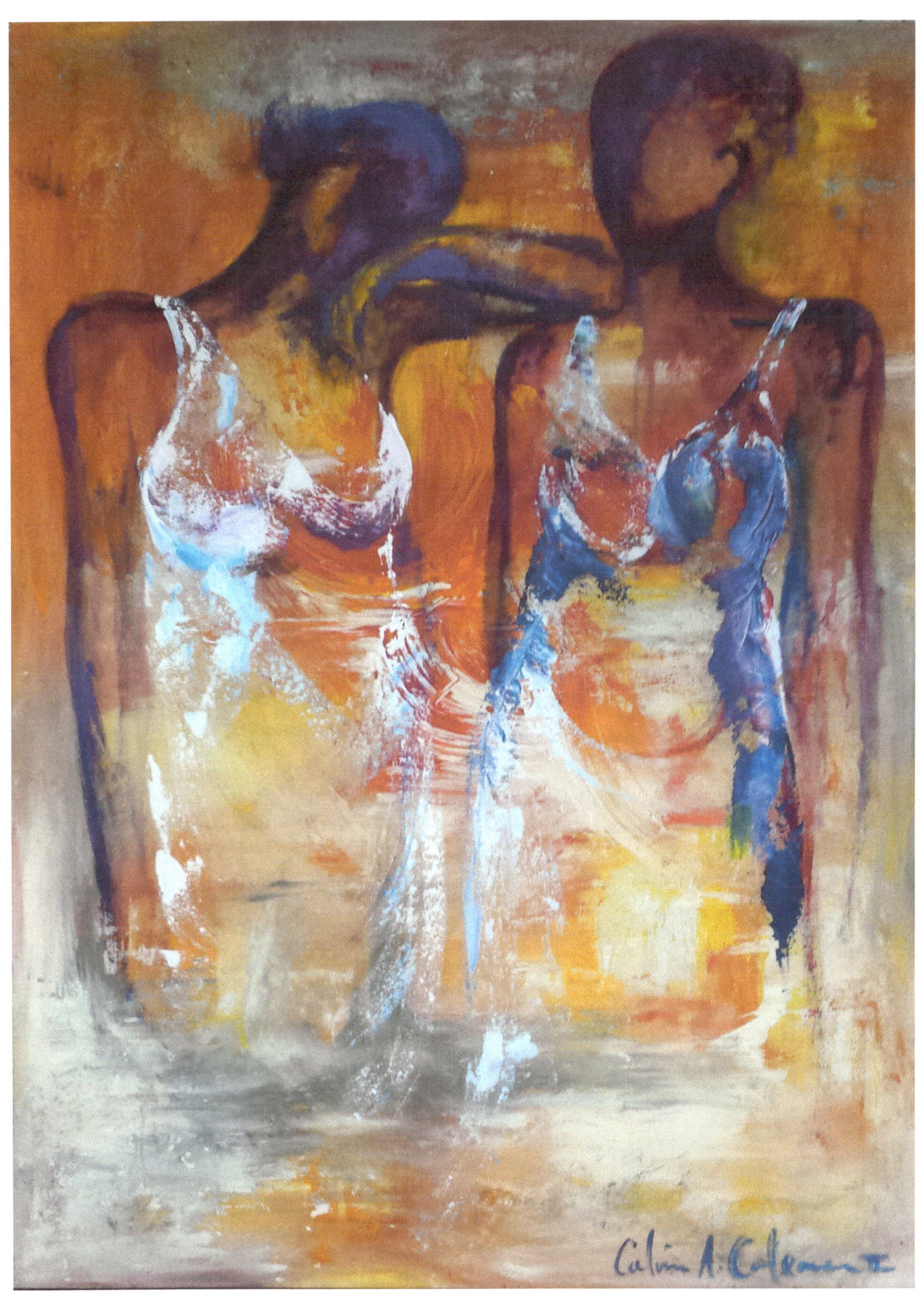
Calvin A. Coleman II

BALLERINA

I have always enjoyed and admired the fluidity of ballerinas who are typically graceful, mobile, and poetry in motion. My goal was to capture the grace of a ballerina showcasing her energy and her softness.

30in x 20in
Acrylic Mixed Media on Canvas

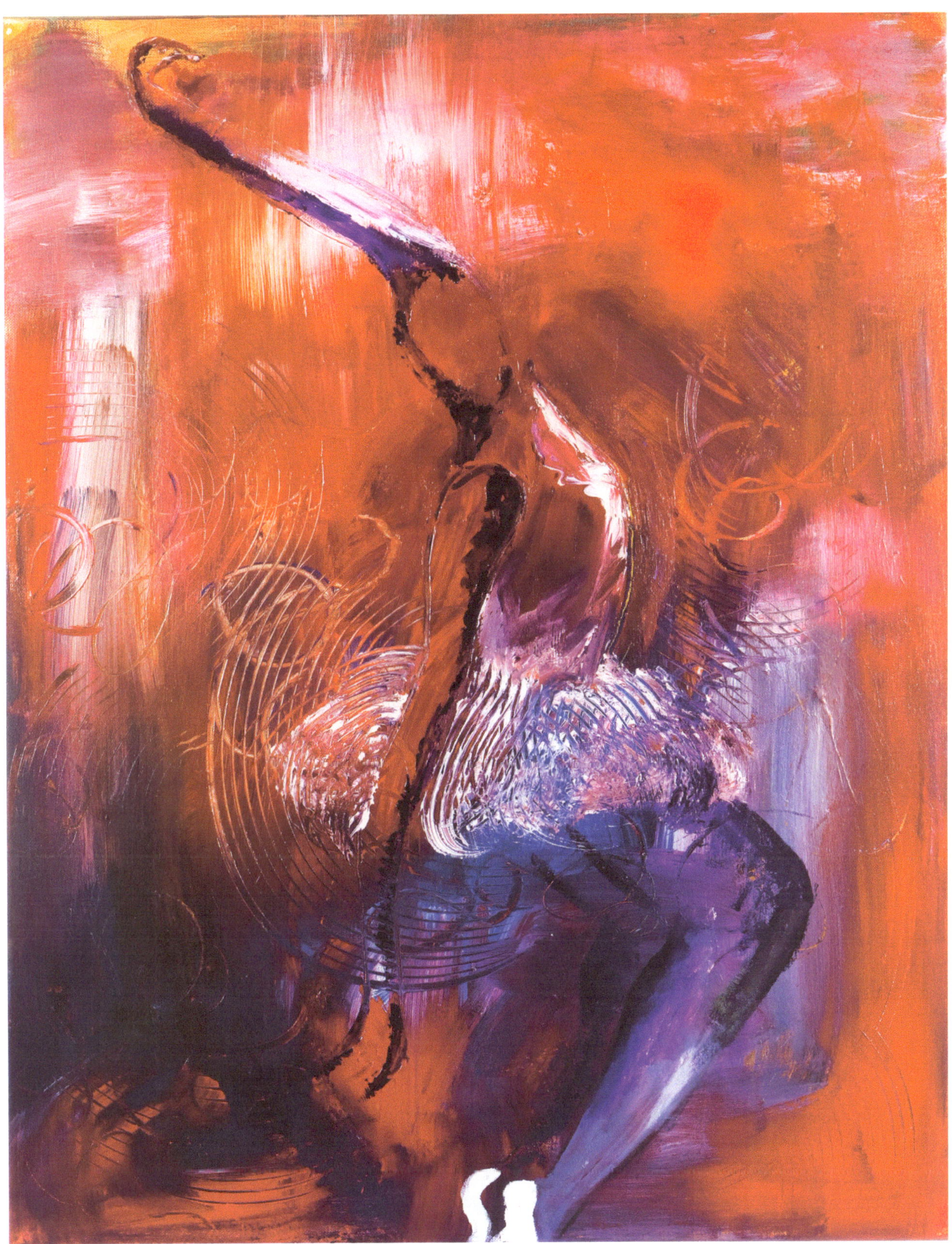

MOTHER AND CHILD

When I study the work of Elizabeth Catlett, I am moved by the scenes that depict a mother's love and the connection and the unconditional love that exists among family members. I wanted to use my creativity to develop a painting that is similar to her style. This painting is a representation of that work and I consider it to be a tribute to her and her work.

30in x 20in
Acrylic Mixed Media on Canvas

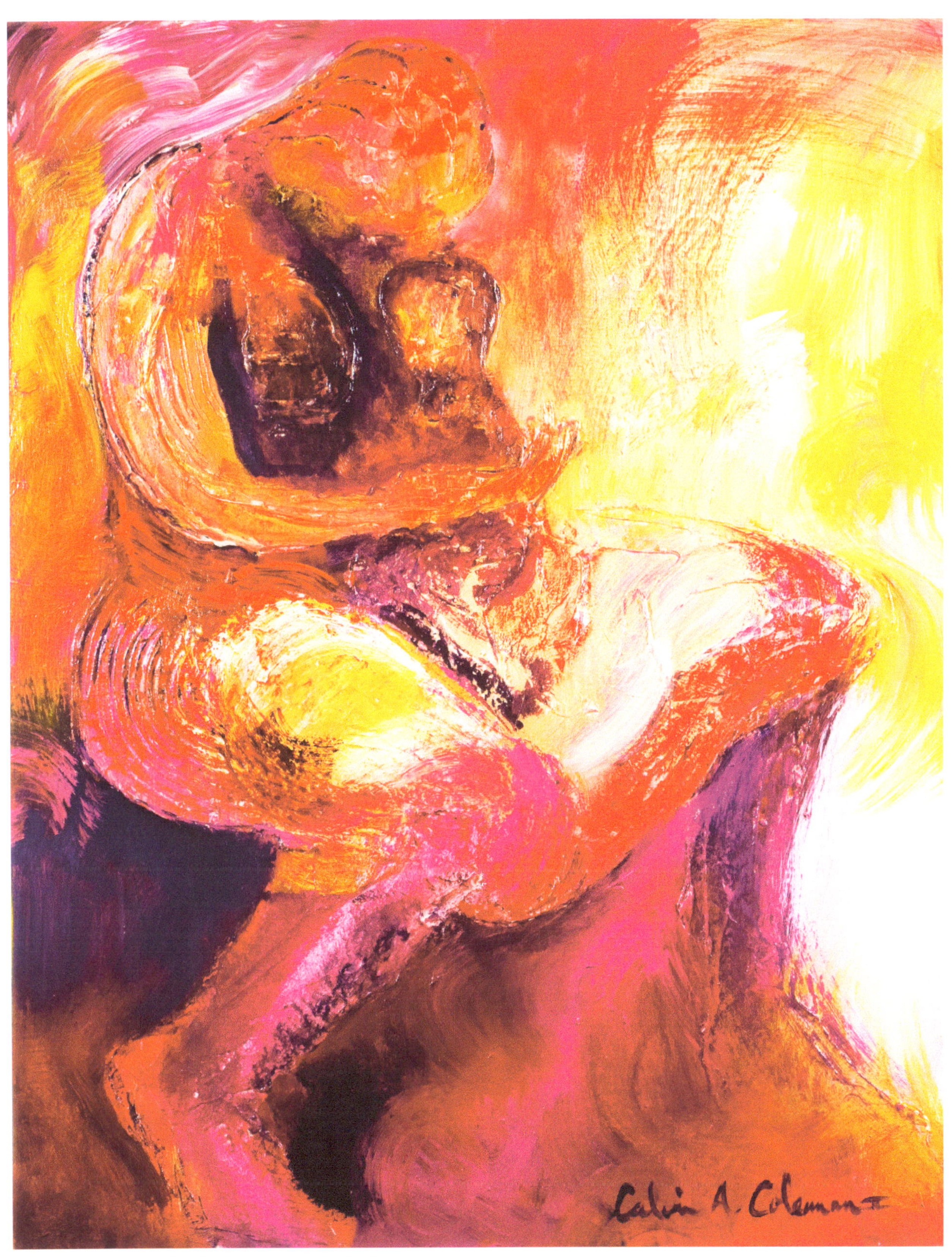
Calvin A. Coleman II

IDENTITY

The purpose of my silhouette style figures is to provide the viewers with an opportunity to see themselves within my work. Without facial characteristics, the subjects could very well be anyone. Although I know how to paint facial details, I deliberately leave them out, in an effort to draw people into my work.

10in x 10in
Acrylic on Canvas

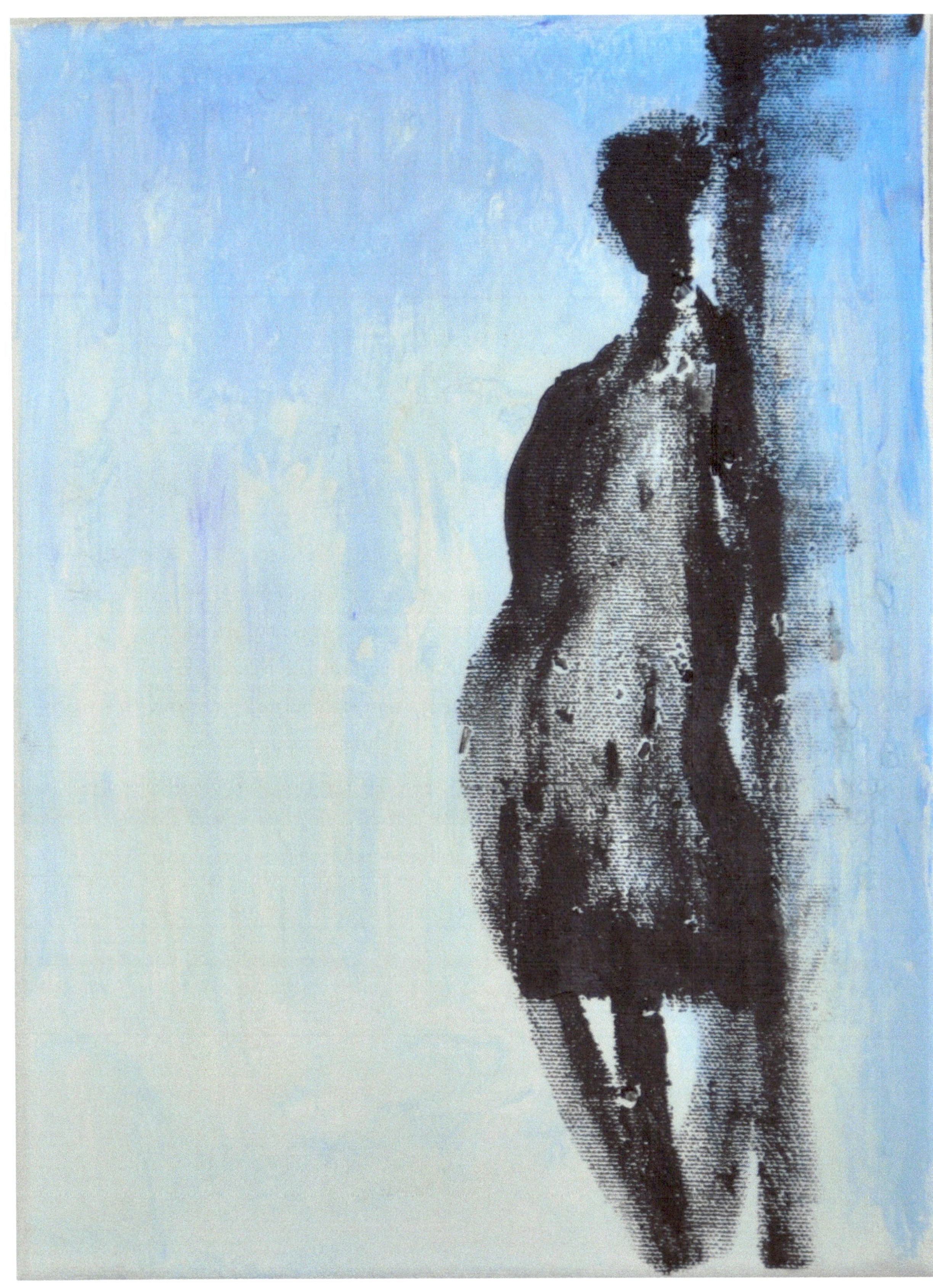

SEATED WOMAN

One of the painting styles that I incorporated in some of my work is when I accentuate certain parts of the subject's body. Sometimes it may be creating the whole body in a large manner and other times it may be certain areas of the body. I have studied the way that Diego Rivera manipulated limbs and body parts. Many of the female figures in his paintings are larger women. At times, I choose to embellish on those same characteristics. In this particular painting of the seated woman, her legs were created a bit larger in scale than the rest of her body. My purpose was to bring attention to that part of the canvas and then allow the viewer to explore the rest of the painting in its entirety.

24in x 18in
Acrylic on Canvas

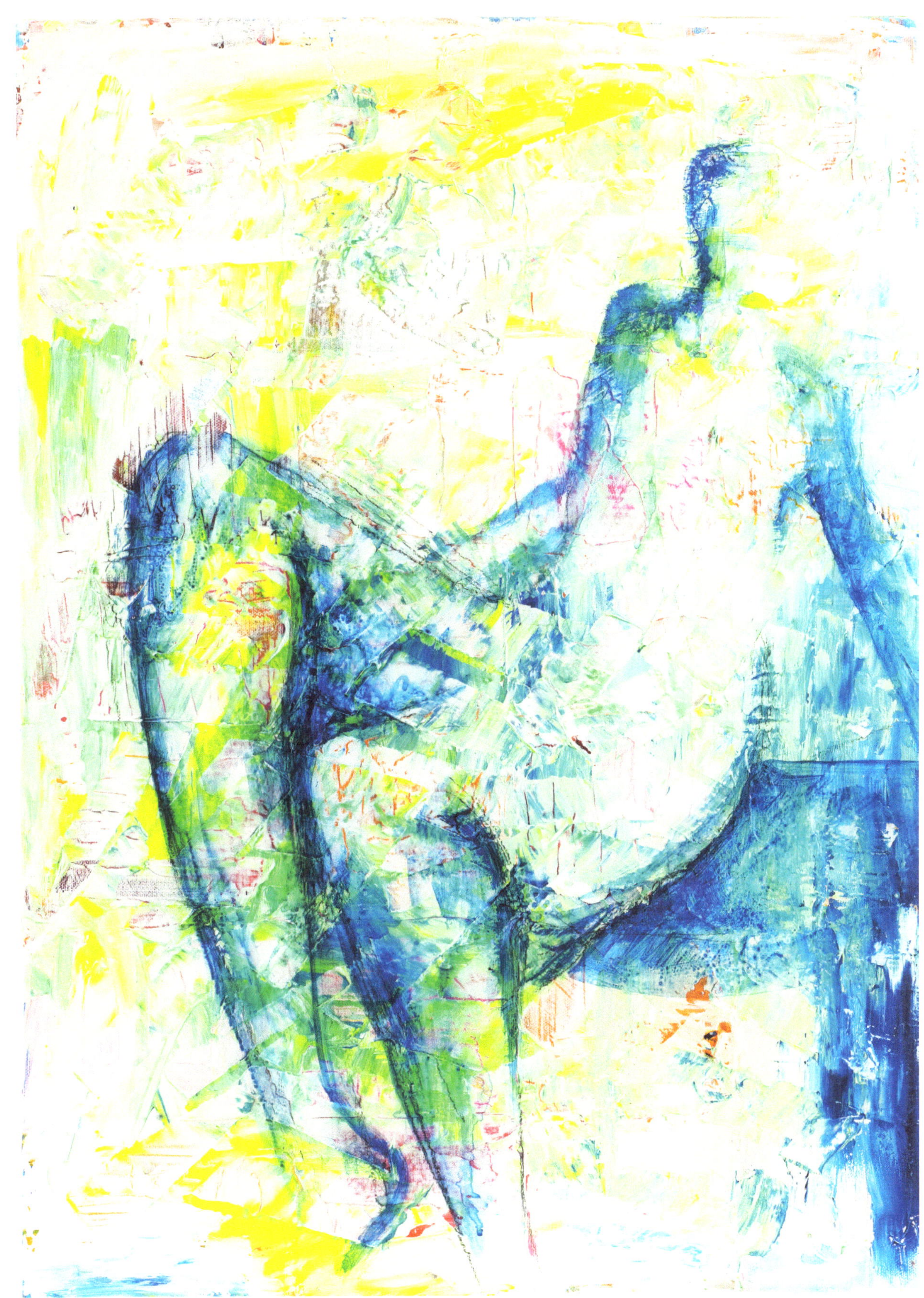

WOMAN WITH FLOWERS

The spirit of giving is a powerful attribute that is an asset to our society. In this painting, I wanted to showcase the power of giving with the gesture of a woman offering flowers. The flowers are representative of beauty and life.

48in x 36in
Acrylic Mixed Media on Canvas

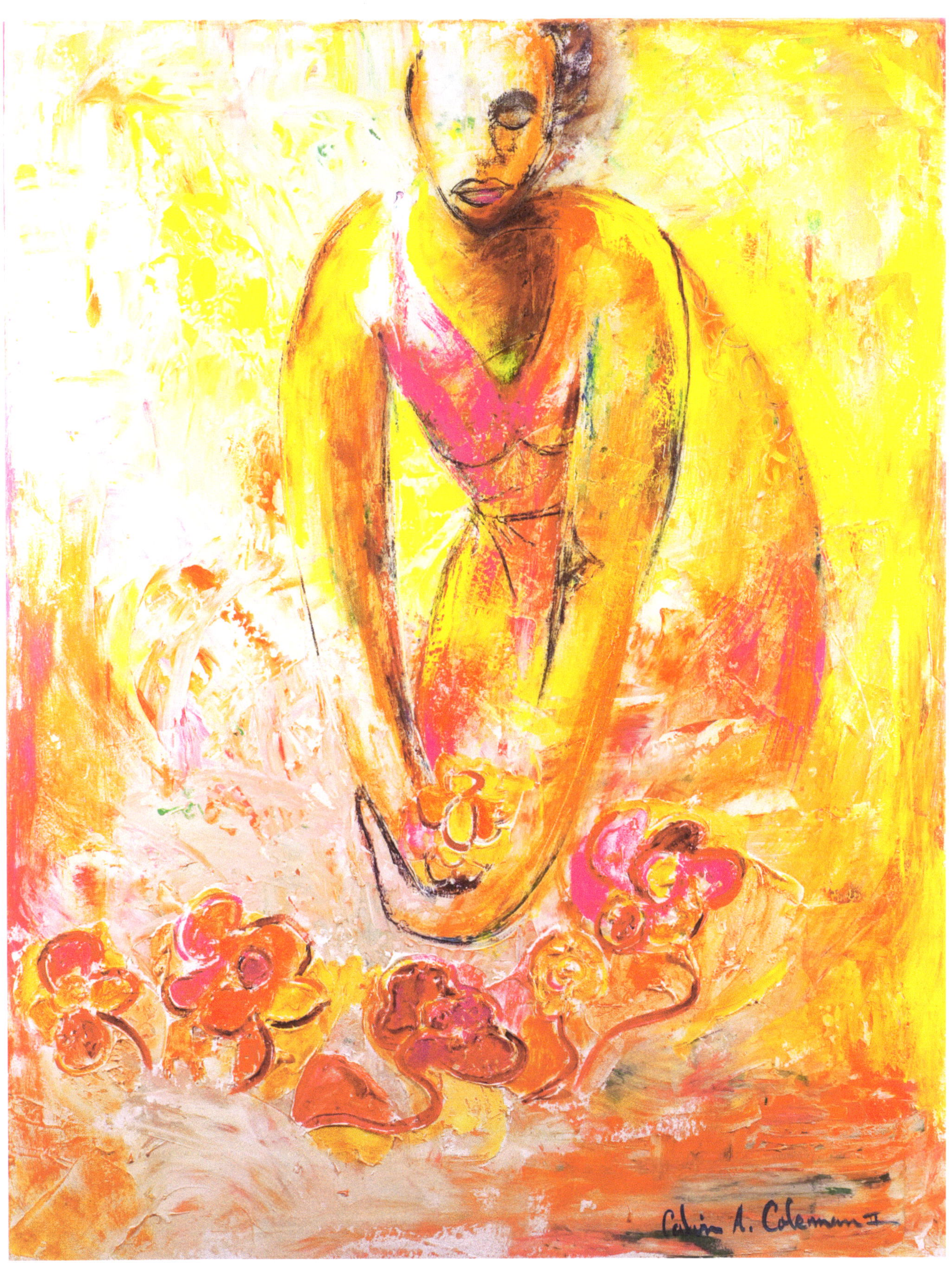
Calvin A. Coleman II

BALLERINA 2

I have always enjoyed watching ballerinas move across the stage and share their gift in a way that is almost surgical in its precision. I wanted to capture a ballerina in motion by accentuating their arms, their flow, and their grace.

30in x 20in
Acrylic Mixed Media on Canvas

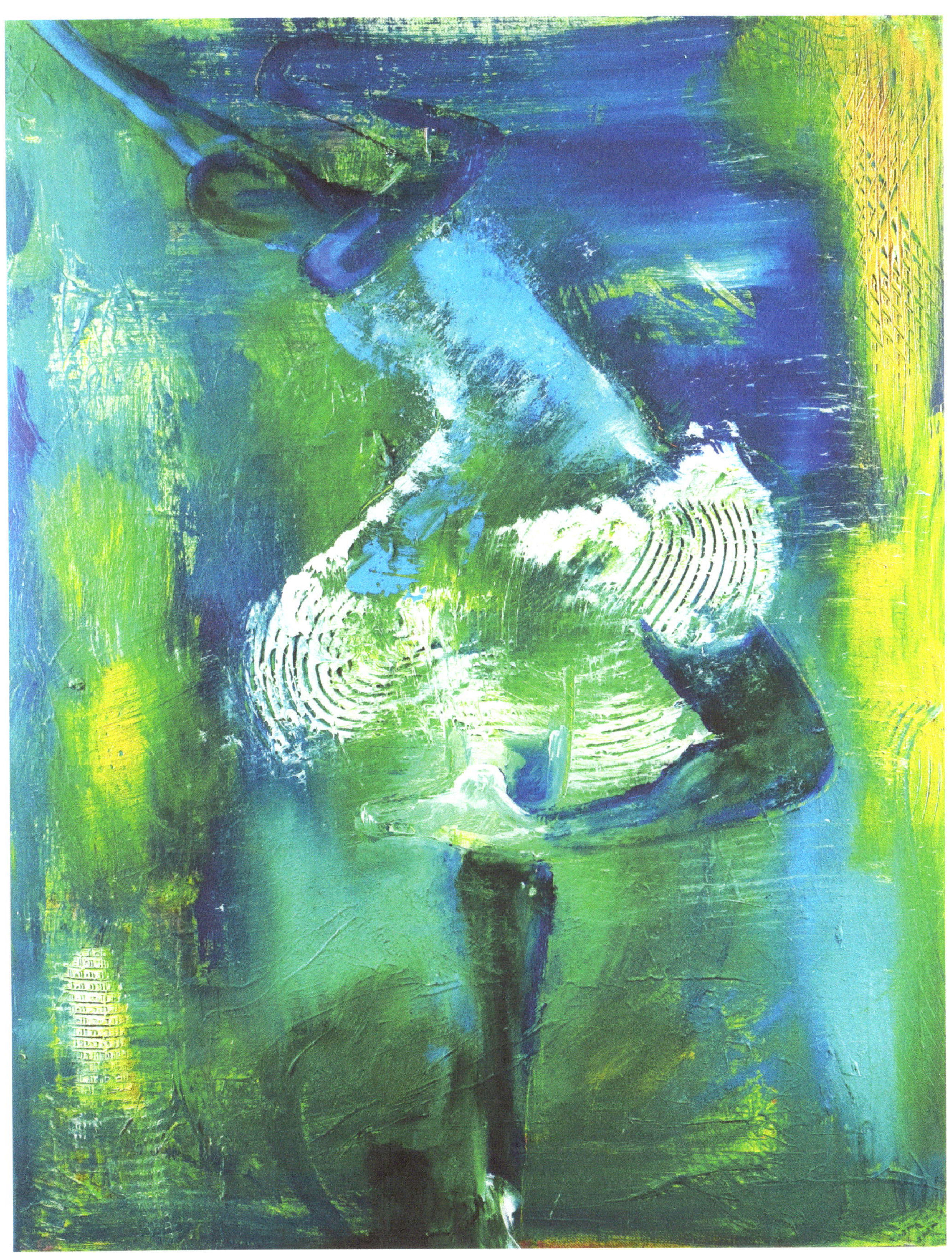

FRUIT IN HER BAG

My goal was for this painting to reflect the true meaning of creativity so I worked to combine abstraction with detail. I wanted there to be a definite distinction in the style of painting on the bag versus the woman who is holding the bag. I purposefully painted her so that she would be obscure yet the viewer would still have a detailed focal point to examine. I call this the "pinball affect," as viewers typically bounce between the bag, the fruit, and the woman to try to get a full understanding of the painting.

48in x 36in
Acrylic Mixed Media on Canvas

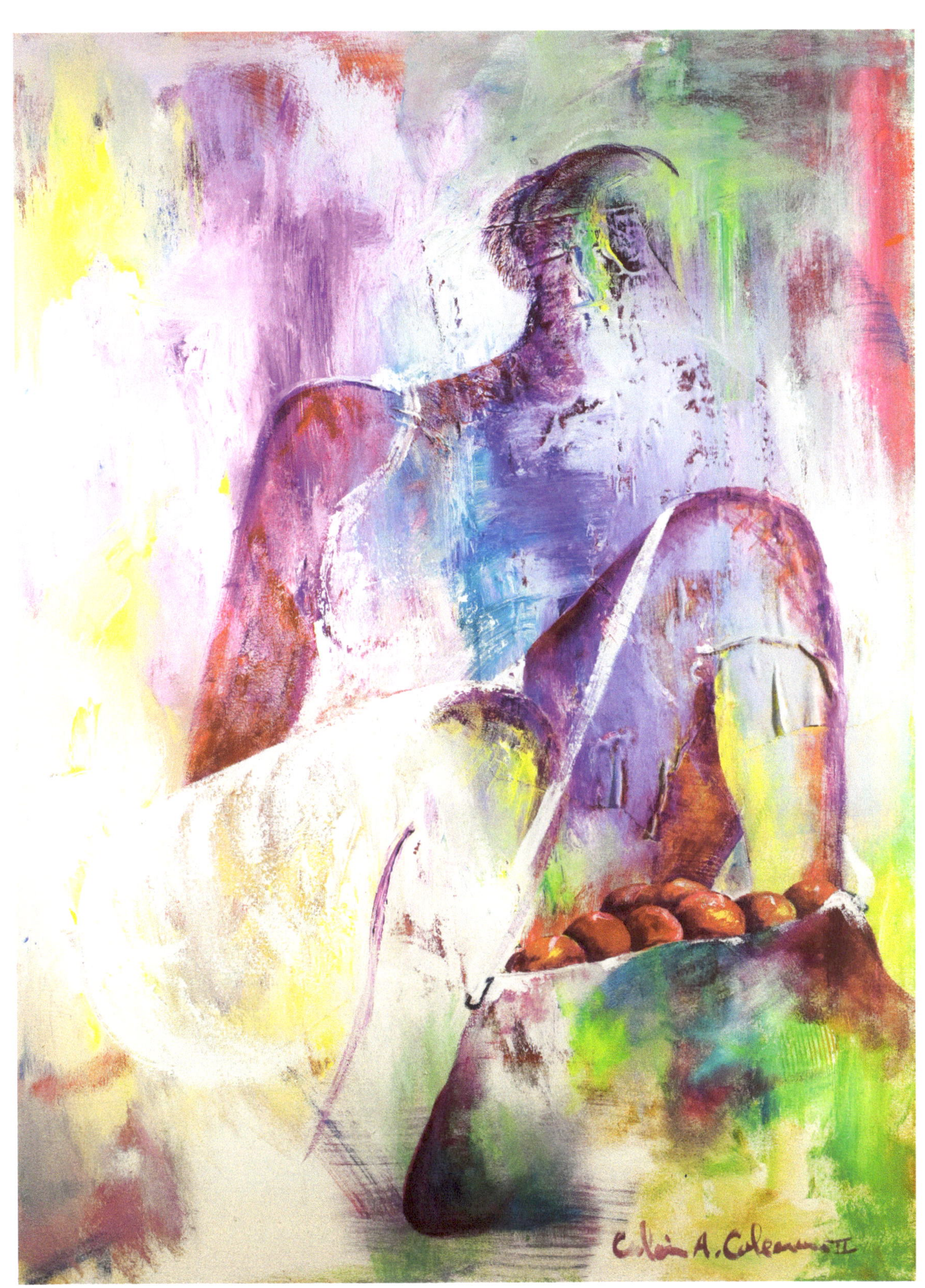

POSE 2

My use of textiles in paintings adds personality to an artwork. The contrast of textured canvas or flat canvas, allows the patterned textile to be an added character to my painting. When I paint on textile, I enjoy manipulating the paint and allowing that particular process to blend into the application of paint on the canvas.

11in x 14in
Acrylic Mixed Media on Canvas

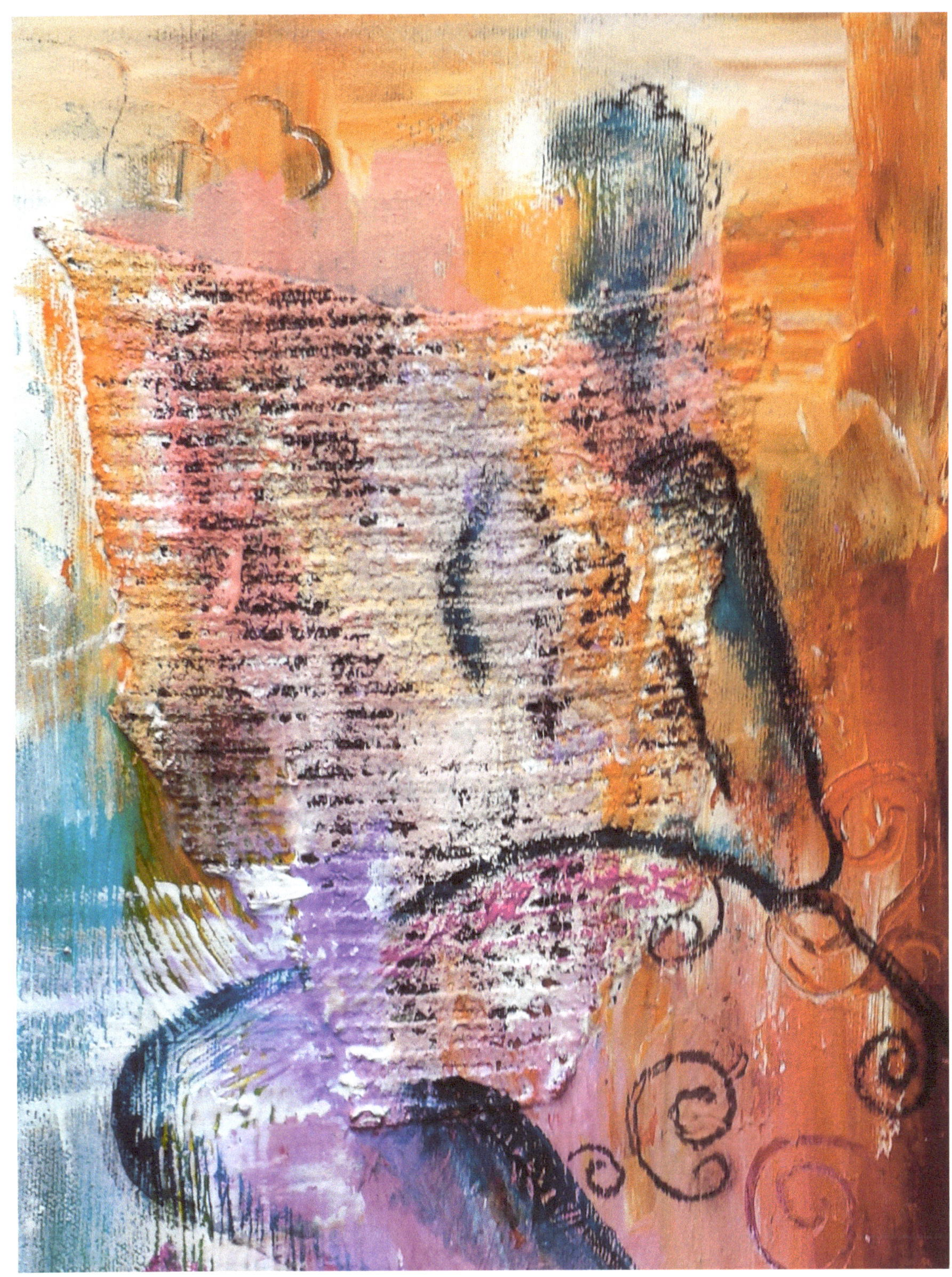

FIELD OF DREAMS

In 2013, I hosted a solo exhibition, "Do You Feel What I See," designed specifically for the visually impaired. Held at the Gallerie Myrtis in Baltimore, each painting was created with texture so that visitors could touch and feel the work. Next to each painting, I included a description of the art in braille. This painting was one of the 32 paintings in the exhibition.

36in x 56in
Acrylic Mixed Media on Canvas

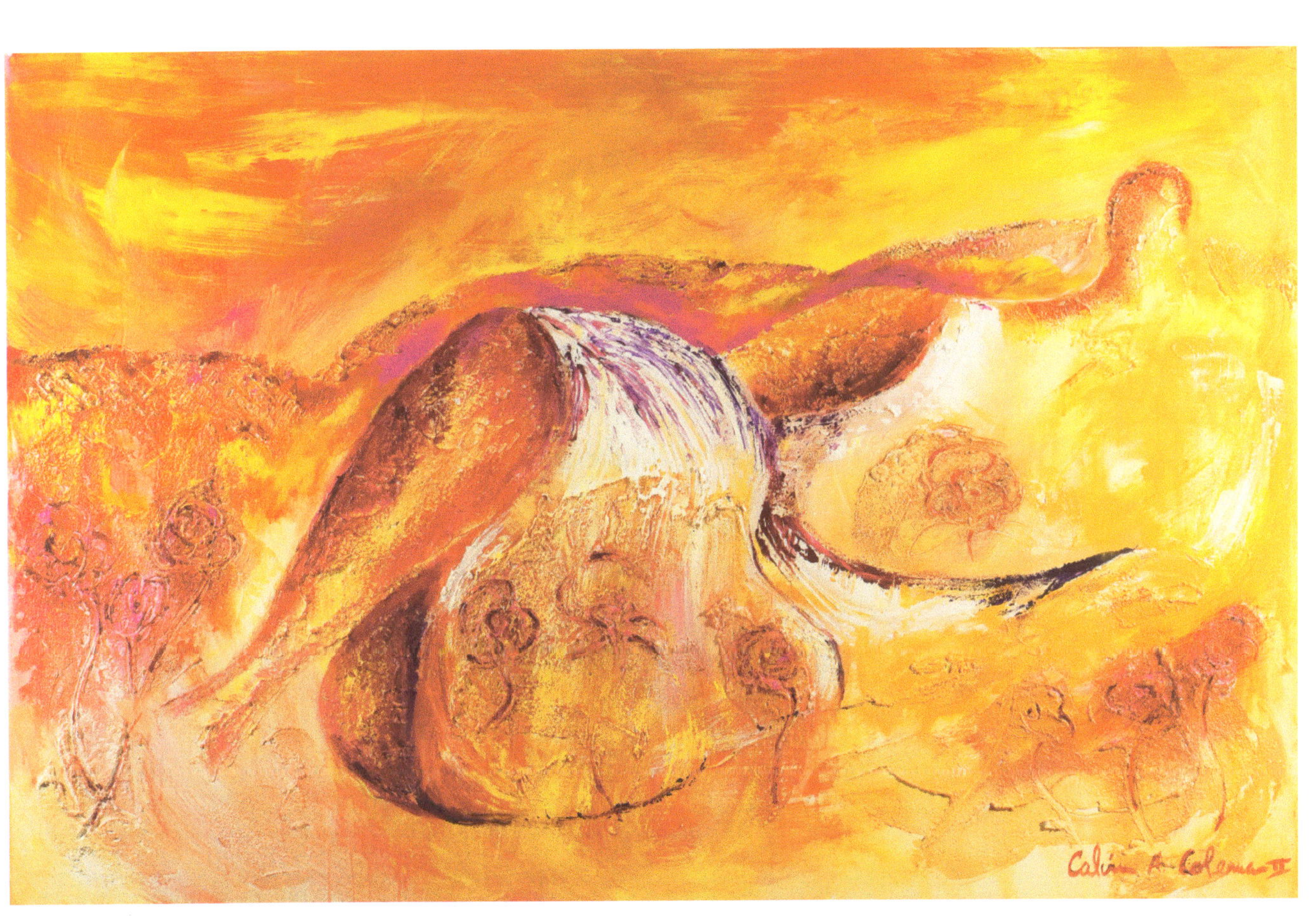

BOUQUET

In many of my paintings, the onlooker typically sees objects and subjects that were not painted intentionally. The question is, do you see one person holding the bouquet or two?

10in x 10in
Acrylic on Canvas

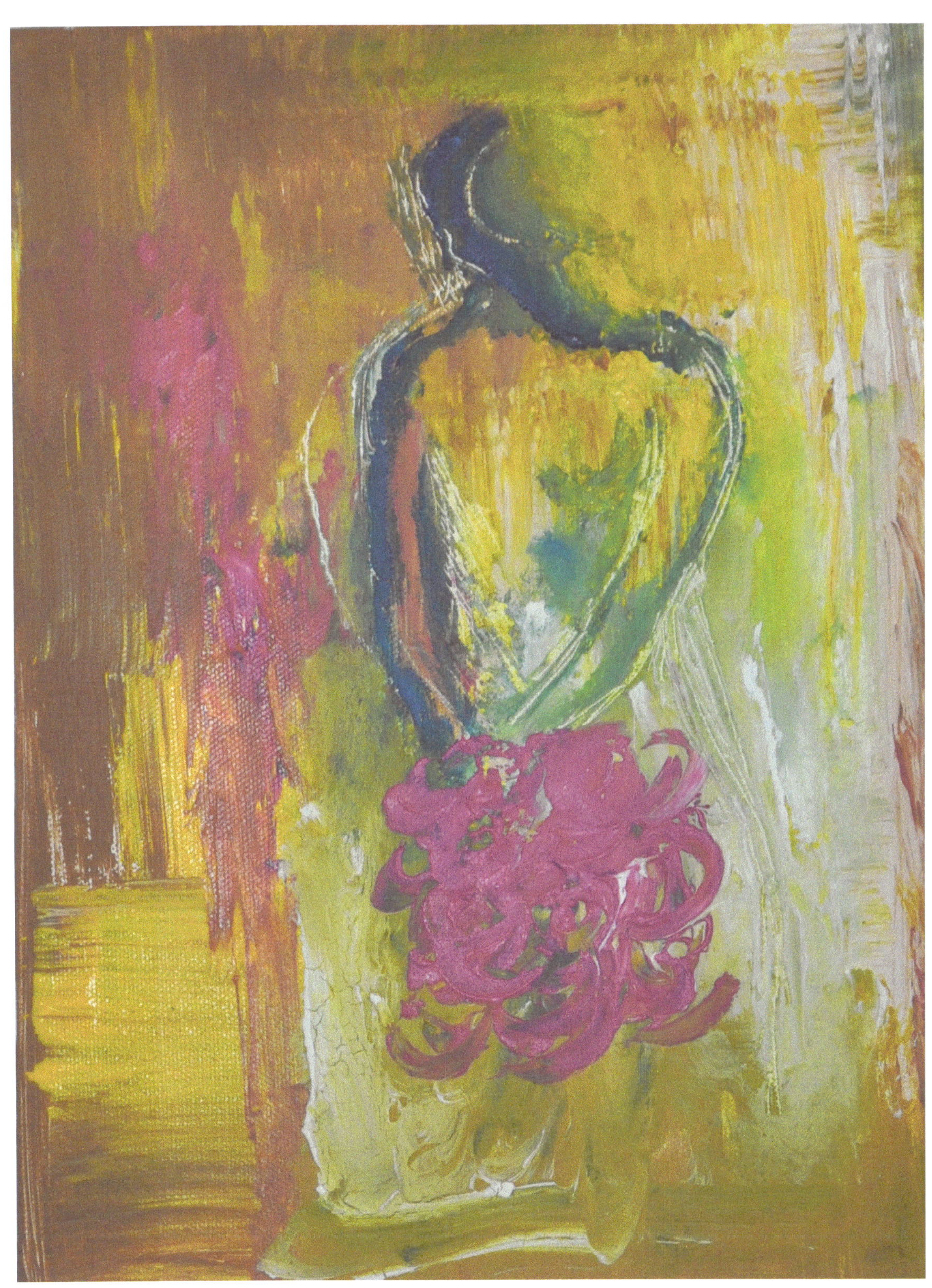

SUBJECT 13

I often paint with ambiguity. This allows the painting to be interpreted in an open-ended way. Painting with mystery is a conversation starter.

10in x 10in
Acrylic on Canvas

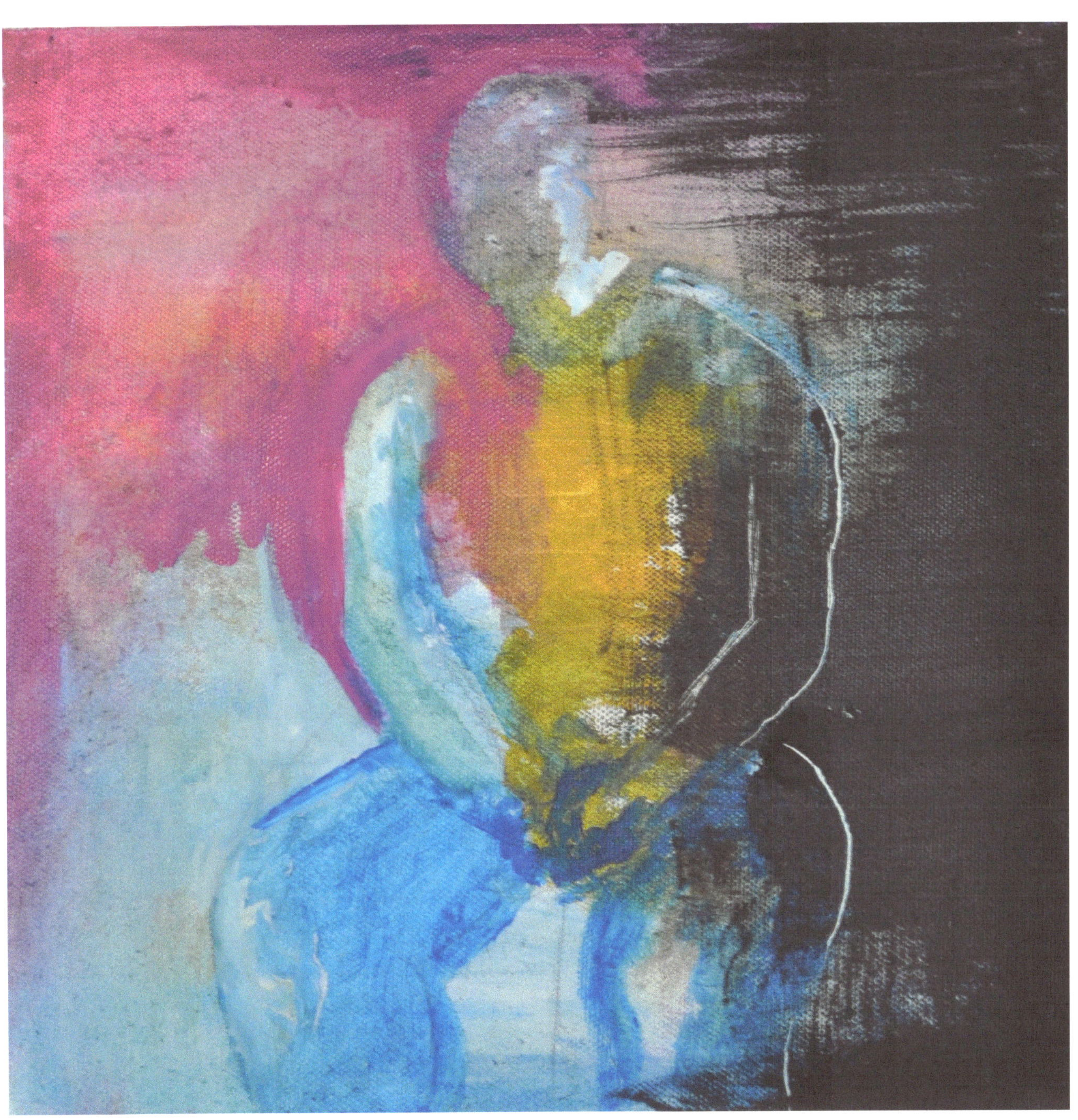

BOND

A mother and her child, is a subject that is often depicted in many different ways for artists. I chose to paint them because of the bond and love that can be displayed through connecting and blending colors.

20in x 16in
Acrylic on Canvas

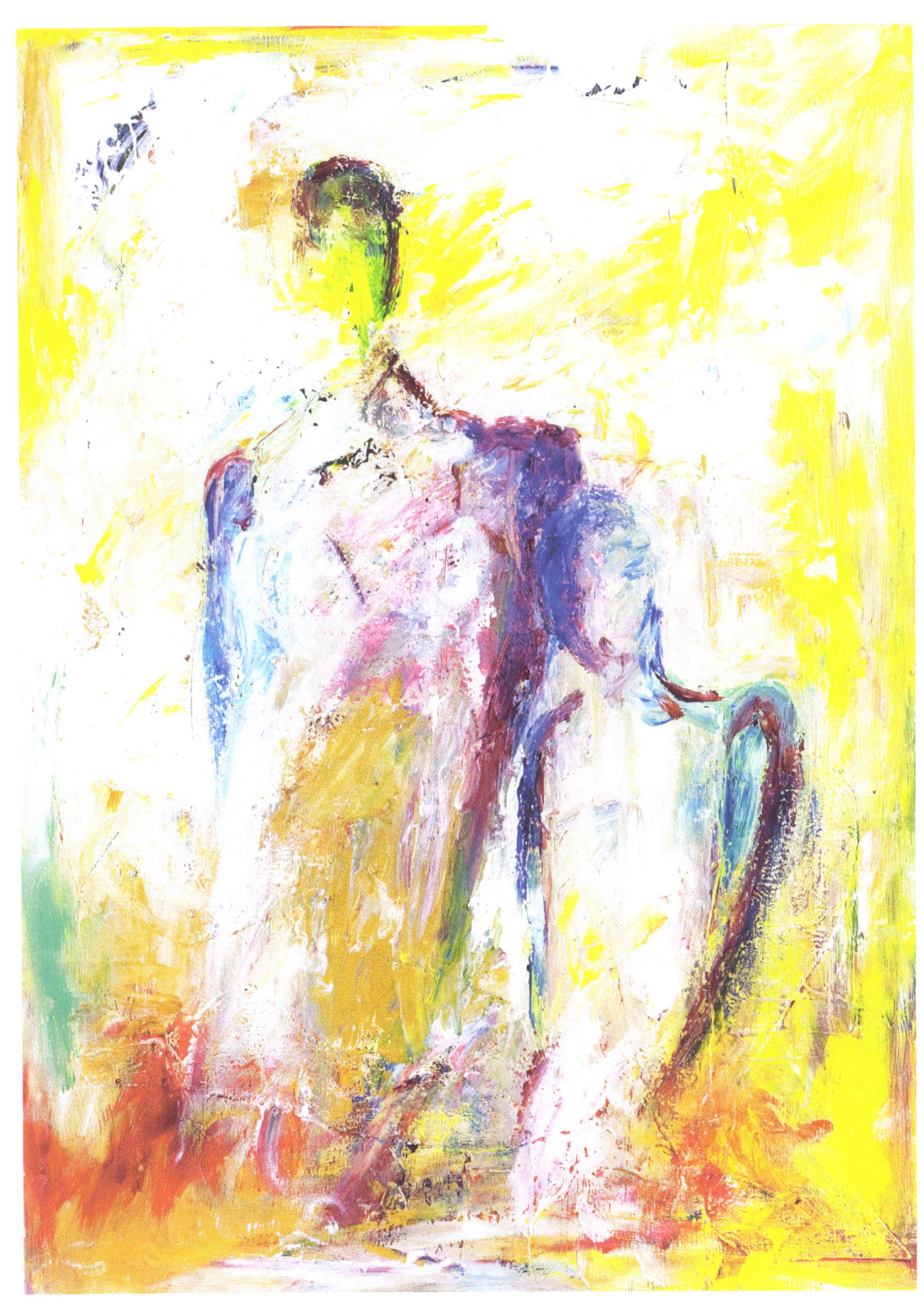

NANA USED TO SAY…

(Experiencing the Work of Calvin Coleman)

When I was growing up my grandmother used to drag me to museums and we would spend hours walking through the halls, staring at each of the paintings and sculptures, searching for the deeper meaning of life. She was in love with the work of Elizabeth Catlett, Charles White, Jacob Lawrence, Romare Bearden, and Henry Ossawa Tanner. She would talk about their work for hours at a time; about the way they were able to use their hands, their eyes, their creativity, and their tools to create something beautiful and meaningful. Art, she said, taught her that when you go beyond the borders and choose to color outside of the lines; and, when you refuse to be average and decide to dream out loud and in color; your genius is sparked, your interest in piqued, and you have the amazing ability to create the world that you want to live in. When I was in college, she would call me whenever she discovered a new artist or attended an opening show. She almost cried when she saw Edgar Dega's "Little Dancer" facing away from the sun or when she realized that a studio director had placed a Frida Kahlo next to a Diego Revera. She said her heart sang when she purchased her first Elizabeth Catlett and sat it directly across from her Charles White. She believed that something special happened when you were in the presence of talent. It was that work, she would sigh and say, that took your breath away and made your hands shake. It made your heart skip a beat and made your soul wonder, while time lost all meaning.

Feelings that she described but I had never really experienced until the day I discovered the work of Calvin Coleman. I must have sat for hours staring at the computer, studying painting after painting, as I searched for the deeper meaning of life. I could not believe what I was seeing. Calvin Coleman is pure raw talent, a genius with a paintbrush and a blank canvas. It is hard to experience his work and not be moved. His book deserves to be on every coffee table, comfortably resting under one of his paintings. His work is amazing on canvas and absolutely unbelievable in person. It is an investment, one that will sit on your wall until that day when you make your grandchild stare at it for hours, in the hope that they will find the deeper meaning of life.

—Karsonya Wise Whitehead • *Baltimore, MD*

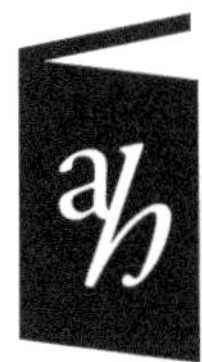

Apprentice House is the country's only campus-based, student-staffed book publishing company. Directed by professors and industry professionals, it is a nonprofit activity of the Communication Department at Loyola University Maryland.

Using state-of-the-art technology and an experiential learning model of education, Apprentice House publishes books in untraditional ways. This dual responsibility as publishers and educators creates an unprecedented collaborative environment among faculty and students, while teaching tomorrow's editors, designers, and marketers.

Outside of class, progress on book projects is carried forth by the AH Book Publishing Club, a co-curricular campus organization supported by Loyola University Maryland's Office of Student Activities.

Eclectic and provocative, Apprentice House titles intend to entertain as well as spark dialogue on a variety of topics. Financial contributions to sustain the press's work are welcomed. Contributions are tax deductible to the fullest extent allowed by the IRS.

To learn more about Apprentice House books or to obtain submission guidelines, please visit www.apprenticehouse.com.

Apprentice House
Communication Department
Loyola University Maryland
4501 N. Charles Street
Baltimore, MD 21210
Ph: 410-617-5265 • Fax: 410-617-2198
info@apprenticehouse.com • www.apprenticehouse.com

www.ingramcontent.com/pod-product-compliance
Lightning Source LLC
LaVergne TN
LVHW071632100826
845154LV00008BA/138
9781627201094